A POPULAR DICTIONARY OF

Paganism

JOANNE PEARSON

RoutledgeCurzon
Taylor & Francis Group

First published 2002
by RoutledgeCurzon
11 New Fetter Lane, London EC4P 4EE

Simultaneously published in the USA and Canada
by RoutledgeCurzon
29 West 35th Street, New York, NY 10001

RoutledgeCurzon is an imprint of the Taylor & Francis Group

© 2002 Joanne Pearson

Typeset in Times by LaserScript Ltd, Mitcham, Surrey

Printed and bound in Great Britain by
MPG Books Ltd, Bodmin

British Library Cataloguing in Publication Data
A catalogue record of this book is available from the British Library

Library of Congress Cataloguing in Publication Data
A catalogue record for this book has been requested

ISBN 0–7007–1619–X (Hbk)
ISBN 0–7007–1591–6 (Pbk)

#59503339

Contents

Acknowledgements

In compiling this dictionary I was helped greatly by many academic colleagues and Pagan friends, who found the time to help out with problems and to point me in the right direction in search of resources and references. Special thanks are due to Professor Ronald Hutton of Bristol University, who kindly allowed me to read his entries on Gerald Gardner and Alex Sanders for the *Dictionary of National Biography* prior to publication, and has provided a wealth of information and encouragement over the years. Professor Geoffrey Samuel of the University of Newcastle, New South Wales, kindly read and commented on entries related to Hindu tantra, for which I am exceptionally grateful. Marion Bowman, Vivianne Crowley, Jez Green, Graham Harvey, Dominic Montserrat, Robert Poole, and Kate Ward must also be mentioned for their willingness to share information, point out factual inaccuracy, and read entries. Any remaining errors are, of course, entirely my responsibility.

I am, as always, indebted to Nick Freeman, for his careful reading of drafts of this dictionary, valuable comments and suggestions, and encouragement. Without his stoicism in the face of a study strewn with papers and books for months on end, this book would not have materialised!

Introduction

Paganism is an extremely complex phenomenon, arguably not one religion, or 'Paganism', but many 'Paganisms', a coalition which is bound together through significant common ground but which at the same time rejoices both in its contemporary diversity and in the tangles of its historical skein. Even in its modern setting, Paganism has no known or uncontested starting point and no single founder or originator; rather, it has developed into its present forms from a variety of sources which are themselves traceable through the mythic landscape of European history. But the boundaries cannot be set so easily, for Paganism has also drawn upon concepts indigenous to religions outside Europe (adopting chakras from India, for example) and the very word 'Pagan' continues to be an arena of contested meaning.

In contemporary scholarship, Pagan is a term used to describe a variety of contemporary traditions and practices which revere nature as sacred, ensouled or alive, draw on pagan religions of the past, use ritual and myth creatively, share a seasonal cycle of festivals, and tend to be polytheistic, pantheistic and/or duotheistic rather than monotheistic, at least to the extent of accepting the divine as both male and female and thus including both gods and goddesses in their pantheons. It includes a variety of traditions of witchcraft, Pagan Druidry, Asatrú/Heathenism, Pagan shamanism, 'non-aligned' Paganism, some forms of Goddess spirituality, and initiatory Wicca. In a very real sense, then, the term describes a religiosity which embraces a range of different religions, rather than a specific religion. This is in keeping with a generally-held Pagan view that no one belief system is correct, and that each person has the freedom to choose their own religion. As such there are no official doctrines and no central authority. Controversial issues within Paganism thus remain unresolved, and the resulting inconsistencies and conflicts tend to be regarded as both constructive and destructive: whilst some demand that all Pagans take up eco-activism, for instance, others maintain a more *laissez-faire* attitude which expects each individual to practice their form of Paganism according to their own deeply held convictions. The forum for discussions of pertinent issues tends to be the pages of journals and magazines devoted to a Pagan readership, such as the journal of the Pagan Federation, *Pagan Dawn*. The Pagan Federation, the largest umbrella organisation for Paganism in Europe, has set out three principles which it asks members to adhere to:

> Love for and kinship with nature: rather than the more customary attitude of aggression and domination over Nature; reverence for the life force and its ever-renewing cycles of life and death.
>
> The Pagan Ethic: 'Do what thou wilt, but harm none'. This is a positive morality, not a list of thou-shalt-nots. Each individual is responsible for discovering his or her own true nature and developing it fully, in harmony with the outer world.
>
> The concept of the Goddess and God as expressions of the Divine reality; an active participation in the cosmic dance of the Goddess and God, female and male, rather than suppression of either the female or the male principle.
>
> *(The Pagan Federation 1992 p. 4)*

Such principles purposefully allow for a wide range of interpretation, and require the individual to seek out for themselves the ethical codes by which they live.

Such a description of Paganism leads one to draw the conclusion that there are many 'Paganisms' – indeed, that there are as many Paganisms as there are Pagans! However, although there are Pagans who operate in a solitary capacity, Paganism is for the most part a sociable form of spirituality which attracts people who wish to join together in groups. These groups take many forms, from Wiccan covens to Druid groves, from Heathen hearths to magical lodges, and entry into them may be by formal rituals of initiation, dedication to a particular deity or deities, or simply through friendship. Some groups may extol the efficacy of operative magic, deeming it to be a requisite part of Paganism, whilst others eschew magic and follow instead a path of different inclination. But there is common ground as well. Apart from the brief definition provided above, the vast majority of Pagans involve themselves in rituals, the most well-known and extensively celebrated of which are the eight seasonal festivals which together constitute the mythic-ritual cycle known as The Wheel of the Year. These festivals are the so-called Celtic fire festivals or cross quarter days of Imbolc/Candlemas (c. February 2nd), Beltane (c. April 30th), Lughnasadh/Lammas (c. July 31st), and Samhain/Hallowe'en (c. October 31st), plus the

Winter and Summer Solstices (December c. 21st and June c. 21st) and the Spring and Autumn equinoxes (March c. 21st and September c. 21st).[1] Rites of passage for the birth of a new child, menarche, manhood, marriage, menopause, ageing and death are becoming more popular, and of course there are also initiation rituals and those which celebrate the phases of the moon. Inspiration for these rituals, and the authenticity required to legitimate them, is drawn from the ancient past discovered through archaeology, classics, myth and history, for Pagan religions tend to trace their roots back to the traditions of ancient paganism, reviving and recreating their practices and beliefs in the context of modern-day life. Indeed, the word 'Pagan' itself has been part of this reconstruction.

Three meanings have been attributed to the word 'pagan' (Hutton 1999), all of which have influenced contemporary Paganism and its self-definition. In the first meaning, 'pagan' is taken to refer to 'country-dweller', an interpretation which seems to have developed mainly with the Romantic literature of the late eighteenth and early nineteenth centuries, and Victorian urban growth from the mid-nineteenth century. Romantic literature combined in varying degrees philhellenism, nostalgia for a vanished past, or *saudade* for an unknown one, and desire for organic unity between people, culture and nature (Hutton 1999: 21), its main enthusiasts in England being poets such as John Keats and Percy Bysshe Shelley. By the mid-nineteenth century, towns had grown at a rate which led some to celebrate nature as a form of resistance to its perceived disappearance. According to the UK Census of 1851, for example, the English urban population outnumbered the rural for the first time. Between 1821 and 1841, the population of London rose by 20%, Manchester, Leeds and Sheffield increased by 40%, while that of Bradford rose by a spectacular 65% (Williams 1975: 188). It has been suggested that this growth of urban areas during the Victorian era caused 'an almost hysterical celebration of rural England' from the 1870s onwards, with the Arcadian goat-god Pan being invoked as great god of nature and the idea of the Greek goddess Gaia as Mother Nature and Mother Earth becoming popular (Hutton 1996: 9).

The growing interest in the environment, and the urge to leave behind the towns and cities and enter once more into communion with 'nature' as 'the countryside' encouraged popular usage of the term 'pagan' as one who dwells in the rustic areas, and the engagement of poets and authors with nature and the countryside certainly influenced the development of

---

1 In the southern hemisphere, the dates are reversed so that Imbolc falls on 1st August and Lammas on 1st February, the Summer Solstice on 21st June and the Winter Solstice on 21st December etc.

Wicca and then Paganism. However, it is the very growth of the city which accounts for what is a primarily urban phenomena – most Pagans live in towns and cities – at the same time as it provides a focus for discontent and an opposition to idealised nature.

The veneration of nature in modern Paganism, the concern for the earth as deity, and the pantheism of seeing the divine in all of nature has led modern Pagans to maintain an attitude of reverence for the wild, untamed countryside on the one hand, and of sadness or revulsion at human estrangement from this ideal, living in towns and cities away from the land, on the other. For some Pagans, veneration of nature and identification as 'Pagan' manifests as a romantic attachment to the countryside, a dream of living away from the towns and nurturing a closer relationship with nature; but it has been pointed out that, 'most [Pagans] are urban, as is usually true of those who love nature (the farmers are too busy fighting it)' (Russell 1991: 171). For others, direct action against the destruction of the environment – at road protests, proposed building sites, or simply to protect an old tree – is the favoured means of expressing their concern for nature and their belief that nature is divine, ensouled, or at the very least, alive. Others see nature as all-inclusive, regarding all that we do as 'natural' for we, as humans, are also part of nature.

However, most town-dwellers were in fact pagan at the time the term 'pagan' was coined. Thabit ibn Qurra, a Sabian from Harran (835–901 C.E.) praised ancient paganism to the Caliph of Baghdad with the words:

> Who else have civilised the world, and built the cities, if not the nobles and kings of Paganism? ... They have filled the earth with settled forms of government, and with wisdom, which is the highest good. Without Paganism the world would be empty and miserable.
>
> *(Thabit ibn Qurra, in Scott 1985: 105)*

This clearly has nothing to do with a rustic existence, and by the early fifth century, *pagani* was used by Christians simply to refer to those who were not members of their own religion. Since resistance to Christianity in late antiquity was led by the nobility and academics, it is highly unlikely that 'pagan' was used to relate to religions exclusively of the countryfolk.

This brings us to the second meaning, that of 'civilian' (Fox 1986: 30–31). By the second and third centuries, the *pagani* were those who had not enlisted as part of God's 'army', as soldiers of Christ against the forces of Satan. Among early Christians, *pagani* thus came to be used to distinguish the *militia Christi* from mere 'civilians'. This meaning, however, died out by about the fourth century. By this time, the pagans were simply those who had not yet received baptism, and the term seems to have been used objectively as a term of identification rather than as a pejorative term of contempt. 'Pagan' as 'civilian', as one not enlisted in the 'army of God', expresses the synonymity of 'pagan' with 'heretic' in the popular mind, sometimes as non-Christian and often as anti-Christian. Undoubtedly, many Pagans today see themselves as opposing Christianity, identifying with the persecution of witches in early modern Europe by the Christian Church, and reacting against the patriarchal, monotheistic religion of Western culture.

Such an attitude of 'being Pagan' in opposition to 'being Christian' is not, however, ubiquitous. Many Pagans claim to be tolerant and respectful towards other religions and spiritual practices. Much changed in the 1990s, as the influence of historical research permeated Paganism and historical claims were re-evaluated. Along with this re-evaluation of the past has come a re-evaluation of Christianity. Wiccans and Pagans are involved in the development of interfaith meetings with members of other religions, and as Paganism has grown in popularity, and public awareness of it has increased, it has adopted a less reactive posture which no longer requires legitimisation through false histories or hatred of the Christian Church.

Pierre Chuvin's third, and most widely accepted definition of the word 'pagan', however, challenges both of these earlier derivations, arguing that pagan simply referred to 'those who preferred the faith of the *pagus*, the local unit of government; that is, the rooted or old, religion' (Hutton, 1999: 4), rather than the new universal Christianity. Thus, by the sixth century, *pagani* had indeed come to mean 'non-Christian'. The interpretation of 'pagan' as a follower of the religion of the locality is becoming more noticeable among modern Pagans, who perceive themselves to be creating links with the energy of the land at a local level, celebrating their rituals with reverence for the *genius loci*, the spirit of the place, or with gods and goddesses traditionally associated with a locale. A recent account of Pagan Druidry by Emma Restall Orr, Joint Chief of the British Druid Order, expresses this interpretation of Paganism as local religion:

> [Paganism] is a religion of locality. i.e. it is where the devotees revere the spirits of the landscape around them, the water courses and wells on which they depend, the soil of the fields and forests that surround them, the sprites and elementals, sometimes to deification. It is a basic attitude in the Pagan mentality that the spirit of the land is the most potent force.
>
> *(Restall Orr 1998: 140)*

The term 'pagan' can thus be interpreted according to all three definitions provided above, indicating 'country-dweller', non-Christian, and the religion of the locality. The latter interpretation is, however, by far the most popular among modern Pagans, who are well aware of their own and ancient pagans' urban rather than rustic existence, and who are reluctant to define themselves in terms of reference to Christianity.

There is, however, a central problem in the usage of the word Pagan: not only is its meaning contested, but its usage is diverse causing a range of problems of identification. The conflation of ancient paganism (whether factual or imagined) with contemporary Pagan practice has led scholars and some practitioners to differentiate between the two by using either capitalisation or prefixes. Some scholars thus refer to contemporary Pagans and Paganism with a capital 'P', and use lower case to denote ancient paganism. In North America and continental Europe, 'Neopaganism' (or any other permutation of capitalisation and hyphenation – neo-Paganism, Neo-Paganism etc.) is the preferred term in academic circles, in order to differentiate between the paganism of the ancient world and modern Paganism.

However, this prefix is not universally applied, particularly in Britain, and the term is contested by both academics and practitioners. Practitioners, for example, have often assumed that context makes it apparent whether they are talking about their own contemporary practices or ancient Græco-Roman worship, and some regard the prefix 'neo' as dangerous because it is easily associated with 'neo-Nazi'. To others, it is felt to lead to questions of authenticity as people equate it with 'quasi', or it is regarded as a trivializing modifier and thus disrespectful. On the other hand, many scholars use the term not only to distinguish between ancient and modern pagans, but also between broken, or disrupted, religious traditions (e.g. Asatrú, Druidry) and unbroken, or continuous ones (e.g. Hinduism, the traditions of indigenous peoples). Thus, 'neo' is used as an appropriate prefix for discussion of those modern-day traditions which are based on a re-interpretation of old traditions which can only be partially reconstructed from archaeology, books, folklore, history, mythology and other sources. 'Pagan' may therefore be seen as a general term for such religions, old and new, but it can be divided for academic purposes.

One practitioner, Isaac Bonewits, has in fact suggested broadening the spectrum using the prefixes 'paleo', 'meso', and 'neo'. According to his definitions, 'Paleopaganism' refers to original tribal faiths found in Europe, Africa, Asia, the Americas, and Australia, plus Hinduism, Shinto, and Taoism. 'Mesopaganism' refers to those religions founded as attempts to recreate, revive or continue what their founders thought of as the paleo-pagan ways of their ancestors before being heavily influenced by Christianity, Judaism and Islam, and include some Druidry and classical, early Wicca. 'Neopagan' refers to those religions created since 1960, blending what their founders perceived as the best aspects of different types of paleopaganism with modern Aquarian age ideals, whilst attempting to eliminate western monotheism and dualism. They include the Church of All Worlds, traditions of Wicca derived from classical Alexandrian/Gardnerian, Goddess spirituality, and feminist witchcraft.

Unfortunately the nature of such boundaries remains arbitrary and somewhat artificial, with groups moving from the 'Meso' to the 'Neo' category, whilst claiming to be 'Paleo'! However, with the growing differentiation of the varieties of Paganism, it might become possible to retain the use of 'Pagan' (as context specific and thus requiring no prefix) when discussing such traditions whilst at the same time being aware that there are practitioners who refer to themselves as 'Pagan' without reference to any specific group such as Wicca or Druidry. On the other hand, as scholarly work continues in this area, it may finally be decided to refer to each specific group, of which 'Pagan' would be one alongside Wicca, Druidry etc. In this case, 'Pagan' would indeed become a specific religion rather than an all-embracing term used to denote a type of religiosity or spirituality.

Further confusion derives from earlier usage. The word 'pagan' still remains in the Oxford English Dictionary as a descriptive term for anyone who is non-Christian or non-Christian, Jewish, or Muslim, and has been applied not only to indigenous peoples but also to atheists, agnostics, and hedonists. To some degree, it is still understood in this sense by many people. Neopagan, on the other hand, was used in a rather derisory fashion by Virginia Woolf from 1911 to describe Rupert Brooke's circle of friends who embodied the rural myth of nude bathing and free love (as a principle, if not in practice) in a pastoral idealism equated with innocence, the Arcadian promised land, in the Edwardian era.

To a certain extent, then, two types of Paganism can be traced, as interpretations of (1) the classical ancient world and (2) the religious and magical beliefs and practices of indigenous peoples. From the first are derived both the traditions of high ceremonial magic to be found within the Western Esoteric Tradition and the regard for nature popular amongst those honouring the ancient Greeks in the nineteenth century. Both influence Paganism, but to a degree it is Wicca which has retained greater evidence of the former whilst other forms of Paganism have tended to emphasise the latter. From the second are derived the assimilation of Eastern ideas within Theosophy, for example, and the later, post-1960s love-affair with the East, plus the appropriation of indigenous spiritual practices. It is, on the whole, Pagan groups such as feminist witchcraft and

Druidry which make use of techniques borrowed from indigenous peoples, such as medicine wheels, sweatlodges, vision quests, and deities such as Yemaya.

Given all of the above, it may seem redundant to point out that the process of selecting entries for this dictionary has not been easy. Sifting through a huge number of possible entries in an attempt to cover the whole field of contemporary Paganism will no doubt have resulted in what some will see as glaring omissions. Contrary to this, there will be some terms which may seem to have no place in a dictionary of Paganism, or which even seem incompatible. Heathens, for example, often do not regard themselves as 'Pagan', yet Heathen terms are included. Likewise, ritual magic is not necessarily Pagan, but its history is entwined with the development of Paganism and it is thus hoped that the inclusion of terms and people related to ritual magic will prove of use. Nevertheless, as the principle argument of this introduction has shown, there is a great deal of difficulty in drawing the boundaries around Paganism, in deciding where Paganism ends and its borrowings from other traditions begin. Thus, concepts such as 'chakra' are included only in the sense in which they are used by contemporary Pagans and because they have been adopted and adapted by Pagans, not because they are intrinsically Pagan in themselves. For similar reasons, I have not gone into great detail about the history of such terms, for this volume cannot set out to cover entries in the considerable length of an encyclopaedia. Issues of conflict and debate are likewise described all too briefly.

From the lexicon of mythology and pantheons I have mentioned only a few names, in order to give a flavour of their importance within Paganism; the reader who wishes to know more is directed to the numerous encyclopaedias of mythology which abound. The selection of terms, peoples, and places contained in this volume will seem arbitrary, but my aim has to been to pick out only those which occur frequently in Pagan literature and which will thus, I hope, prove useful to the general reader. Some of the terms are relatively unknown outside of Paganism and its study, and so wherever possible I have tried to trace the derivation of words such as 'athame', even though there is no proven etymology.

One last limitation must be set before the reader. Although there is now a great range of books available on Paganism, from practitioner accounts to DIY to scholarly studies, there remains the issue of secrecy and access to oath-bound material for any writer. This is particularly relevant to Wicca, and thus has an effect on the dictionary as a whole. The upsurge in published works on Paganism obviously mitigates the problem to a certain extent, but it is always necessary to respect people's wishes not to read their lives laid out in print, and to willingly exclude from publication that material which is considered oath-bound. Lastly, it is in the nature of mystery religions to contain mystery, and it is impossible to convey the sense of that mystery in a short dictionary entry. Whilst practitioners might claim that one can only engage with the mysteries by experiencing them, the reader is directed to the select bibliography at the end of the dictionary, where a number of books may give at least a sense of such experience. For this reason, the bibliography includes works by both practitioners and academics and will, I hope, prove useful to both the scholar and the general reader.

It is my aim in this dictionary to provide an overview of Paganism for all who may need to refer to it, so that those with little or no knowledge of Paganism can grasp at least its basic tenets and concepts. I hope it may prove useful in the ongoing exploration and understanding of this rich and colourful phenomenon.

Blessed Be!

References

Bonewits, Isaac (1979/1997), *Defining Paganism: Paleo-, Meso-, and Neo-*, www.pagansonline.com/~bonewits/PaganDefs.html.

Chuvin, Pierre (1990), *A Chronicle of the Last Pagans*, Cambridge, MA: Harvard University Press.

Fox, Robin Lane (1988), *Pagans and Christians in the Mediterranean world from the second century AD to the conversion of Constantine,* Harmondsworth: Penguin.

Hutton, Ronald (1999), *The Triumph of the Moon: A History of Modern Pagan Witchcraft*, Oxford: Oxford University Press.

Hutton, Ronald (1996), 'The Roots of Modern Paganism', in: Harvey, Graham & Charlotte Hardman (eds), *Paganism Today: Wiccans, Druids, the Goddess and Ancient Earth Traditions for the Twenty-First Century*, London: Thorsons, 3–15.

Restall Orr, Emma (1998), *Spirits of the Sacred Grove: The World of a Druid Priestess*, London: Thorsons.

Russell, Jeffrey B. ([1980], 1991), *A History of Witchcraft: Sorcerers, Heretics and Pagans,* London: Thames & Hudson.

Scott, Walter (ed.) (1985), *Hermetica: the Ancient Greek and Latin Writings which contain Religious or Philosophical Teachings ascribed to Hermes Trimegistus,* Boston: Shambala.

Williams, Raymond (1975), *The Country and the City*, St. Albans: Paladin.

A Popular Dictionary
of
Paganism

A

AA See *Argenteum Astrum*.

Abra-Melin Magic *The Sacred Book of Abramelin the Mage* was claimed to have been written in three volumes in 1458 by Abraham the Jew, who travelled to Egypt in search of teachers of secret traditions and became a pupil of Abramelin in Arachi. He collected his knowledge in this book, which was translated into French around 1700 and became part of a manuscript in the Bibliothèque de l'Arsenal in Paris. This was the version read by Eliphas Lévi and translated by S. L. MacGregor Mathers. Its central principle is that the material world is created by evil spirits directed by angels, and claims that all humans have an angel and a demon in attendance. It instructs the magician on the magical operations necessary for contacting their Holy Guardian Angel, lists angels and demons who can be invoked for specific purposes, and contains magic squares which can be used for invisibility, flight, command of spirits, necromancy, and shapeshifting. Aleister Crowley was fascinated by this book and spent a long time preparing to perform the Abramelin magic, for which purpose he bought Boleskine Lodge near Loch Ness.

adept A person who is considered to be highly proficient in a particular body of occult lore and practices.

Adler, Margot Grand-daughter of psychologist Alfred Adler, Margot Adler compiled one of the first substantial surveys of paganism, published in 1979, and revised and expanded in 1986, as *Drawing Down the Moon: Witches, Druids, Goddess-Worshippers, and Other Pagans in America Today*. She is an initiate of Gardnerian Wicca, having become interested in witchcraft through her lifelong interest in Greek mythology.

Æ See *Russell, George*.

Aesir In Norse mythology, the chief race of deities including the pantheon of sky gods and goddesses, such as the chief god Odin, Frigga, Thor and Baldur. The Aesir live in the realm of Asgard, and war against their enemies the frost giants. See also *Asatrú; Asatrú Free Assembly; Vanir*.

Aether   In Greek myth, Aether is the son of Nyx (night) and Erebus (darkness). His name means 'brightness', and personifies the upper air where the light was thought to be brighter and clearer than in the air immediately surrounding the earth. In modern Wicca and Paganism, aether is regarded as the fifth element of spirit, which is not of the mundane world but exists rather as that 'brighter and clearer air' of Greek mythology. Spirit leads the four mundane elements of earth, water, fire and air. It is also used sometimes as an alternative name for the astral realm, and is sometimes called quintessence.

AFA   See *Asatrú Free Assembly*.

Agrippa, Henricus Cornelius   (1486–1539) Born in the German town of Cologne to a family of minor nobility (von Nettesheim), Cornelius Agrippa (as he called himself) spent his life studying magic, Greek philosophy, Jewish Kabbalah, and the works of Hermes Trismegistus, although an ambivalence between Christian and pagan teachings pervaded his life. Agrippa is most famed for his *Three Books of Occult Philosophy*, an encyclopaedia of Renaissance magic the complete version of which was published in Cologne in 1532, and which was plagiarised by Francis Barrett in *The Magus, or Celestial Intelligencer* in 1801. He also wrote a treatise on *The nobility of the female sex and the superiority of women over men* in 1509 (published in 1532), dedicated to Princess Margaret, daughter of Maximilian I and governor of the Netherlands, Burgundy and Charolais. A seeker of truth, Agrippa was horrified by the accusation of witchcraft against a peasant woman of Vuoypy, near Metz, and defended her legal rights, sending a letter to the judge overseeing her trial which argued against the 'torturing of harmless women'. As a result of his intervention, the inquisitor was removed from the case, the accused woman granted absolution, and her accusers fined one hundred franks for unjust accusation.

air   Lightest of the four classical elements of nature that form the basis of life (earth, water, fire, air). Often symbolised by the colours blue or yellow and associated with the Greek east wind Eurus, youth, morning, spring, insight, intellect, the athame, and the zodiac signs of Gemini, Libra and Aquarius. Along with fire, air is considered to be a masculine element.

Alban   The ancient name for Scotland.

Alban Arthuan   ('the light of Arthur') Druidic name for the Winter Solstice.

Alban Eiler ('the light of the Earth') Druidic name for the Spring Equinox.

Alban Elued ('light of the Water') Druidic name for the Autumn Equinox.

Alban Heruin ('light of the shore') Druidic name for the Summer Solstice.

Albion The ancient name for England.

alchemy An ancient mixture of chemistry and spirituality the purpose of which was to find the philosopher's stone or elixir of life which would grant immortality. The word is derived from the old name of Egypt, Khem, and the practice grew largely from Gnostic texts on metallurgy dating from the second century, and later from texts which came to light via the Arab world whence the *Corpus Hermeticum* arrived in Europe in the late fifteenth century. It was immensely popular in Christian Europe between 1400 and 1700, with eminent scientists such as Boyle and Newton committed to its quest. Jung did much to revive interest in alchemy in the twentieth century, and in Paganism it tends to be regarded as an analogy of the search for the true self, for the grail, symbolised in previous eras by the attempt to transmute base metal into gold.

Alexandrian Wicca Type of Wicca named after Alex Sanders, who founded his own style in the late 1960s. Alexandrian Wiccans are those whose initiatory lines descend from Alex and Maxine Sanders. It remains one of the main forms of Wicca practised today, particularly in Britain. Many Wiccan practices are in fact a synthesis of the Alexandrian and Gardnerian Wicca, and an increasing number of Wiccans are initiated jointly or separately into both traditions, thus tracing their lineage back to both Gardner and Sanders. The differences between the two traditions have been played down, and the similarities and synthesis emphasised to such an extent that some Wiccans claim that there is no difference between them, whilst others retain a 'pure' Gardnerian or Alexandrian practice. Alexandrian Wicca differs from Gardnerian in its emphasis on ceremonial magic, the addition of a formal admission of novices through a neophyte ritual to the three degree system, and second and third degrees being given together, though this is no longer always the case.

Alpha et Omega Occult magical Order and splinter group of the Golden Dawn after its collapse in 1903. Its members included J. W. Brodie-Innes, its leader, and Moina Mathers, and it aimed to preserve the original Golden Dawn concepts. Its demise, along with the other splinter groups, including the Stella Matutina, was heralded by the publication by Israel Regardie of the Golden Dawn rituals.

Amen-Ra Temple   Edinburgh lodge of the Golden Dawn, led by J. W. Brodie-Innes until forced out by MacGregor Mathers.

Amergin, song of   An ancient Celtic calendar alphabet found in Irish and Welsh, said to have been chanted by the chief bard of the Milesian invaders as he stepped onto Irish soil in 1268 BCE. It was restored by Robert Graves in *The White Goddess* (1948) and is very popular in Wiccan and Pagan circles.

American Tradition   A form of Wicca created in 1971 by the founders of the Pagan Way, combining knowledge from various traditions. It was intended to make Wicca more accessible by removing the restrictions enforced by Gardnerian oaths of secrecy.

amulet   A protective charm usually worn around the neck or placed in the home, such as an ankh, scarab, udjat eye, charm bracelet or rune. It is distinct from talismans, which are worn to bring benefit rather than protection.

ancestors   Regarded as important in some Pagan religions, particularly those in North America influenced by Native American Indian spirituality and Mexican traditions, the ancestors are honoured and worshipped at certain times of the year, particularly Samhain (Hallowe'en) when the dead are remembered.

Ancient Druid Order   Organisation founded in London by John Toland in 1717, which influenced the development of other druid orders during the nineteenth century. Its leaders include George Watson McGregor Reid, elected in 1908, who led a successful campaign for the right to worship at Stonehenge. The Druid Order and the British Order of the Universal Bond (London Druid Group) derived from the ADO, and a splinter group under Ross Nichols in 1964 became the Order of Bards, Ovates and Druids (OBOD).

Ancient and Mystical Order Rosae Crucis (AMORC)   Modern North American organisation based in California, claiming Rosicrucian origins and offering teaching through correspondence courses.

Ancient Order of Druids   A non-religious order founded by Henry Hurle in the 1780s as a benevolent society, now an international organisation with various splinter groups.

Anderson, Victor   Founder of the Faery Tradition of Wicca, along with his wife, Cora, and Gwyddion Penderwenn.

angels   Spiritual messengers who act as intermediaries between humans and God. Ranked in legions, angels are usually considered 'good' and demons 'bad'. Occultists such as Emmanuel Swedenborg and Rudolf Steiner claimed to communicate with angels, and the Enochian magic of Dr John Dee and Sir Edward Kelly is based on what they claimed to be Angelic language. The angelic stone, which they used for scrying, was given to them by the angels Raphael and Gabriel.

anima   Jung's term for the female side of the male personality.

animals   Certain animals have long been associated with Paganism and witchcraft, including hares, cats, toads, ravens and crows, owls, and dogs.

animism   The belief that everything is imbued with spirit, including rocks, hills, streams etc. not just animals and humans.

animus   Jung's term for the male side of the female personality.

ankh   Or Key of Life, shown as a looped cross, is the primary symbol of the Egyptian mysteries, meaning 'life or living'. It is a symbol of the Nile and its delta, and of the union of the male (staff) and female (loop) principles, a representation of life itself, eternally renewing. The symbol can be seen in the hands of many depictions of Egyptian gods and goddesses, representing the unity of spirit and matter which cannot be separated – divinity is shown forth in life – and is particularly associated with Isis [Aset], who is herself associated with the life-giving waters of the Nile. The ankh is worn as jewellery by many Pagans and occultists today.

Annwn   Welsh name for the underworld, as found in the *Mabinogion.*

anointing   A practice of smearing the body with flying ointment or anointing oils. Anointing is sometimes performed as a rite of purification in Wicca at the beginning of rituals, where the body is marked with the symbol of the initiate's degree with fingers dipped in aromatic oil. This is also performed at initiations, where the initiate is anointed in the sign of their degree with oil, wine and lips as an act of consecration.

Anubis   Egyptian god of mummification and protector of tombs, usually depicted as a jackal or as a man with the head of a jackal. He was believed to lead the souls of the dead to their judgement in the underworld.

AO   See *Alpha et Omega*.

AOD   See *Ancient Order of Druids*.

Aphrodite   Greek goddess of love and beauty, born of the sea foam, equivalent of Roman Venus and Assyrian Astarte. Believed to teach the value of things, including self-worth.

Apollo   Greek god associated with the sun, poetry, music, archery, prophecy, medicine and pastoral life. Orderly and rational.

Apuleius, Lucius   Writer of the classical story *The Transformations of Lucius, otherwise known as The Golden Ass*, dating from the end of the 2nd century CE, and popular during the Renaissance and in modern Paganism due to its description of the rites of Isis and initiation into these rites.

Aquarian Age   A variant on the concept of the 'New Age', representing the belief that we are moving from the age of Pisces into the age of Aquarius following the precession of the equinoxes. This age, according to adherents, will usher in the characteristics associated with the sun sign Aquarius – freedom, individuality, equality, brotherhood.

Aradia   Daughter of the goddess Diana and her brother Lucifer, sent down to earth to teach Diana's magic to witches; goddess of the witches; particularly influential in modern Wicca due to Charles Godfrey Leland's *Aradia, or the Gospel of the Witches* (1899). Also known as Herodias.

archetypal image   Specific personal and cultural expression of an archetype.

archetype   An image or blueprint from earliest times present in the collective unconscious of the human race, providing a form for the ways in which we apprehend the world. In themselves, irrepresentable but expressed as archetypal images. Some Pagans regard deities as archetypes. See also *Jung, C. G.*

Argenteum Astrum   (Order of the Silver Star) An esoteric magical order founded by Aleister Crowley in 1907 after receiving the text of *Liber al vel Legis*, the Book of the Law, from the spirit Aiwass. Crowley thought this to be the framework for a new religion which would replace Christianity. Its journal *The Equinox* published many of the Golden Dawn's secret rituals between 1909 and 1913.

Arianrhod   Welsh goddess of the Spiral Castle (Caer Arianrhod), thought to exist beyond the Northern Lights or the Pole Star, where souls rest between incarnations.

Artemis   Greek goddess of nature and the moon, mistress of the beasts, twin sister of Apollo.

Arthur   Mythical king of Britain around whom many legends have been woven. Most important in modern Paganism is the idea that Arthur was the last pagan king of Britain before it became completely Christianised, and his reign is therefore seen as a golden age, albeit one of struggle. See also *Glastonbury; Morgan le Fey.*

Asatrú   ('trust in the Aesir') Icelandic term used by Heathens to denote their affinity to the Aesir sky-gods of Norse mythology, and also generally applied to Heathenism, particularly in North America. Practitioners follow the pre-Christian Pagan traditions of Northern Europe, centred around two distinctive groups of Norse divinities, the Aesir sky gods (such as the chief god Odin, Frigga, Thor and Baldur) and the Vanir earth gods (such as Frey and Freya). Asatrú is more male-oriented than some Pagan religions, but Asatrú groups are led by both men and women and both officiate in religious ceremonies. Women played an important role in Norse-Germanic religion as Volvas and Seidkonas, the priestess-practitioners of magic and divination, and the work of a number of women and men on these roles and the myths of Northern Goddesses is leading Odinism into a less male-oriented future. Asatrú was revived in the twentieth century and in 1973 was recognised as an official state religion along with Christianity in Iceland, with the right to conduct legally binding weddings and child namings etc. See also *Hammarens Ordens Sällskap; Odinic Rite; Ring of Troth; Rune Gild-UK.*

Asatrú Free Assembly   American organisation founded by Stephen McNallen in 1972, which tended to keep itself apart from Paganism. Until 1987, it published a quarterly journal, *The Runestone*, and held an annual festival called *The Althing*, but the presence of racist and National Socialist adherents caused the assembly to be disbanded. It was succeeded by the Asatrú Alliance and the Ring of Troth.

Asgard   In Scandinavian mythology, the middle realm of the universe in which dwell the gods.

Ashcroft-Nowicki, Dolores   Well-known and highly respected occultist from Jersey, Director of Studies for the Servants of the Light School of Occult Science which trains people in the Western Mysteries, and author of many publications including *The Ritual Magic Workbook: A Practical Course of Self-Initiation* (1986).

Association of Solitary Hedgewitches (ASH)   Contact organisation established in 1994 as a result of the burgeoning interest in hedgewitch-craft. Solitary Hedgewitches can use the association to make contact with each other in order to share experiences and ideas.

Astarte   Canaanite version of Ishtar, Astarte was chief goddess of Tyre and Sidon. A fertility goddess, she was merged with Asherat and Anat, and with the Egyptian goddess Hathor. Her cult was served by priestesses and spread in the UK as far as London, Carlisle and Northumberland under the Roman occupation. Associated with the planet Venus.

astral plane   A concept from ancient times, important in Blavatsky's Theosophy, and still popular among modern Pagans and occultists. The universe is perceived as existing on many levels of reality, of which the physical world and the astral plane (the closest to the physical world) are the most familiar. The astral plane is sometimes identified with the Summerlands, the realm of the afterlife.

astral projection   The physical body is believed to possess an astral body which survives death, and which can separate itself from the body to visit the astral plane during life with appropriate training.

astrology   The interpretation of the movements and positions of the planets through the celestial sphere as an influence on human affairs. One of the most ancient surviving occult sciences, astrology constitutes one of the three streams of the Western Esoteric Tradition. See *Western Esoteric Tradition*.

Aswynn, Freya (b. 1951) Born in Holland, a well-known authority on Norse magical tradition, initiated into Gardnerian Wicca in 1980 before becoming interested in runes and the cult of Odin. As a priestess of Odin, she has worked to bring greater recognition and power to women involved in Odinism, Asatrú and other Northern Traditions. She is the head of Rune Gild – UK, and author of *Leaves of Yggdrasil* (1990).

athame Ritual knife used in Wicca, which traditionally has a black handle and a double-edged blade inscribed with symbols. The knife is held to be a symbolic representation of the individual Wiccan's power, and is known as 'the true witch's weapon'. It is used in ritual to direct energy in such things as calling the four quarters, purifying salt and water, casting the magic circle, and in cakes and wine. Its uses are thus ceremonial – it is not used to cut anything. The origins of the word are shrouded in mystery, though the knife itself is derived from a description of a ritual knife called an *arthana* in some extant texts of the *Key of Solomon*, and the markings to be placed upon the handle when the knife is consecrated are taken from Mathers' translation of the *Key*, in which the word athame does not appear. Other versions of the *Key* give the black-handled knife the names *arclavo, arclavum, arthanus, athany, artamus* and *arthame*, which is closest to Gardner's version, though it is not known why the 'r' was left out.

Atlantis Bookshop Founded in 1922 by the occultist, author, poet and publisher Michael Houghton, the Atlantis Bookshop is a meeting place for many Pagans and occultists and is situated in Museum Street, London. The basement was transformed into a temple, from which Houghton ran a magical lodge, the Order of the Hidden Masters, and the occult Neptune Press, still in business today, was also run from the premises. The Collins family became the owners in 1962, it was taken over by the Psychic Press in 1989, and in 1995 was purchased by a Pagan. Caroline Wise now runs both the bookshop and the press.

aura A subtle energy field seen as white or coloured light which is believed to surround the body of living beings. The aura changes colour according to the health and mood of a person, and can therefore be read and manipulated for the purposes of healing. Auras have been photographed using Kirlian photography, a procedure for photographing energy fields which was developed by the Russian electrician Semyon Davidovich Kirlian in 1939.

Aurum Solis   A school of high kabbalistic magic founded in England in 1897 by Charles Kingold and George Stanton and revived in 1971, whereupon it was taken to the USA in 1978. Membership is by invitation only.

Autumn Equinox   One of the eight festivals of the Wheel of the Year, celebrated as a late harvest festival when the bounty of the goddess from the hedgerows has been gathered. It is one of two equinoxes (the other being the vernal, or spring equinox) which are fixed astronomically according to the time when the sun crosses the celestial equator and day and night are of equal length. Spring Equinox can be seen as a sexual initiation, whilst Autumn Equinox signifies a union on a mystical level as light and dark are once more in balance. At Spring, the double helix of the spiral of life is physical; at Autumn, the double spiral winds and returns as a symbol of reincarnation, an acknowledgement that all of nature shares in the universal cycle of death and rebirth, Autumn's grain becoming Spring's seed. Through entering this spiral and understanding its mysteries, the God transforms into the Great Mystic, and having conquered death and the tomb he returns to take the Goddess with him into the underworld for the winter. Their union mirrors the coupling at Spring Equinox, but now it is deeper and represents a more complete merging of opposites in the great spiral. In Nature, the fruit drops and everything begins to prepare for the winter rest. Pagans look back over the year so far, at what they have achieved and all they have done, assessing their own harvest in their lives as winter approaches.

Avalon   In Welsh mythology, the kingdom of the dead, the Isle to which King Arthur was conveyed after death and from which he is to return, according to legend. Sometimes regarded as the Land of Fairy and the home of the last vestiges of indigenous British Paganism during the onslaught of Christianity.

Avebury   A major late neolithic henge monument in Wiltshire, believed to be the centre of a complex ritual landscape including a stone avenue, Silbury Hill, chambered tombs and other monuments. Avebury is used extensively by the British Druid Order at festival times.

Awen   The sacred symbol of many of the Druid traditions is that chosen to represent Awen (/|\), signifying the descending form of light, the Three

Rays of Light or Three Pillars of Wisdom, and the three drops of inspiration from the cauldron of Ceridwen, a Welsh Goddess. When placed within a circle, the symbol shows three aspects of deity, Truth, Beauty and Love, operating within the circle of creation, the world. The sun is also used as the symbol of divine light. See also *cauldron, Ceridwen, Taliesin.*

B

Bagahi Rune A rune used most commonly in Wiccan rituals of initiation and at Samhain, whose origin is unclear. It appears in a Medieval manuscript of the thirteenth century, and may be in the Basque language. Many witches believe it to be an invocation of Basque god names.

Bailey, Alice Alice La Trobe-Bateman (later Bailey) claimed to have been contacted by the Tibetan Masters who dwelt in the Himalayas, channelling the Master Djwal Khul, and left the Theosophical Society to set up The Arcane School in 1923. With her husband, she set up the Lucis Trust to publish her works, including the magazine *The Beacon*. Believing in a divine plan for the world, as well as karma, reincarnation, and spiritual hierarchy, Bailey aimed to foster the future world civilisation through uniting people of goodwill in World Goodwill, Triangles, and Units of Service.

Balder In Scandinavian mythology, son of Odin and god of the summer sun, invulnerable to everything except mistletoe with which the god Loki tricked the blind Hödur into killing him.

Bale-Fire A large fire lit on Beltane/May Day, often translated as 'bright fire' and thought to have been dedicated to the Celtic God Bel. It is more likely that the name indicates a fire to ward off evil or baleful influences.

Baltic Paganism With the collapse of the Soviet Union in 1989, Paganism became an integral part of the desire to establish national identities in newly re-emerging countries such as Lithuania, Latvia and Estonia. Baltic Paganism is one of the most active and living traditions of European Paganism; traditional folklore with its record of Pagan deities was used for nationalistic purposes, and as late as 1960 the Soviet authorities abolished Midsummer as a national holiday. Christianity came late to the Baltics and the people proudly retained their Pagan heritage, boasting of being the last Christianized region in Europe. Today, Pagan gatherings attract many thousands of people who believe that participating in the rites of their ancestors is an important part of their cultural heritage.

In Lithuania there is a strong Pagan church and an organisation called Romuva (after the Medieval Lithuanian central pagan temple) which promotes Lithuanian Paganism and is also active amongst the Lithuanian community in the United States. Modern Lithuanian Paganism was formally restored in 1967, repressed by the Soviets in 1971, and tolerated since 1988. A similar organisation operates in Latvia, called Dievturiba, after Dievs the sky-god who, along with Laima, goddess of life, is believed to determine the fate of humans. Its Pagan tradition is known as Dievturi, and its aims are to live in harmony with Nature and other members of society and to follow the will of the Gods. In Baltic Paganism, all of nature is considered sacred and the Earth is regarded as the universal mother. The Baltics have a seasonal cycle of eight festivals – the solstices and equinoxes are celebrated, together with four other festivals important in the agricultural year.

Baphomet   Deity traditionally believed to be secretly worshipped by the Knights Templar. The image of Baphomet as an androgynous, bearded figure, used by the nineteenth century German antiquarian Josef von Hammer-Purgstall in *Mysterium Baphometic Revelatum*, and Eliphas Lévi's winged, androgynous sabbatic goat with a flaming torch between his horns, a star above the eye, female breasts, and goat's hooves are now well-known. He has been adopted by Crowley's OTO and other occult fraternities as a tutelary deity.

Bards   The inspired musicians, storytellers and poets of the Druids, who listen to and memorise poems, songs and stories as carriers of wisdom. Their inspiration is believed to come from the Awen, to which they are open physically, mentally and emotionally to allow the inspiration to flow into and through them.

Barrett, Francis   Author of *The Magus, or Celestial Intelligencer*, published in London in 1801. The book was plagiarised from Cornelius Agrippa's *The Three Books of Occult Philosophy*, and was a major source of information for the Golden Dawn.

Bast   Egyptian goddess of Bubastis, in the Nile delta, protectress against disease and evil spirits and a goddess of music and dance, often depicted with a cat's head and/or with several kittens.

Bel   Celtic pastoral deity associated with light, the sun, and healing. Also known as Bile and Belenus.

belief   A debatable concept within Paganism, since it is deemed to be defunct. Pagans claim not to 'believe' in deities or spirits, but to 'know' them. Belief is thus deemed to be unnecessary.

bells   Often used in rituals of Wicca and high magic to alert the astral plane to the fact that a rite is about to begin, end, or to note specific important points within initiation rituals.

Beltane   One of the four greater sabbats of the Wheel of the Year. Beltane is the Irish gaelic name for the month of May, and is celebrated on May Eve/May Day. Opposite to Samhain on the Wheel, Beltane marks the beginning of summer and good weather, when the cattle could be taken up to the high summer pastures. Rituals to celebrate Beltane reflect the burgeoning fertility of the land, the marriage of the God and Goddess, and the blooming fertility of Nature. The God is represented as recognising his responsibilities to the Goddess; though he is still Lord of the Greenwood, he has committed himself to her and to their child. For some Pagans, this is interpreted as a reflection of the transition from adolescence to adulthood, from animalistic passion to love. Fertility is celebrated by dancing round the maypole, weaving ribbons in a representation of the never-ending spiral of life. In folklore, many customs centre around divination by young women to find out the identity of their future husbands, and divination is still practised as part of modern Pagan rites since, like Samhain, the veil between the worlds is deemed thin and the 'otherworld' is thus accessible through techniques such as scrying.

Benandanti   Fifteenth century fertility cult in Northern Italy which conducted rites to ensure good crops and was outlawed by the inquisition.

Bennett, Allan   (1872–1923) High-ranking member of the Golden Dawn, Mathers' second in command, who became Aleister Crowley's mentor in 1899. He lived in London with Crowley before moving to Ceylon and becoming a Buddhist monk. He eventually settled in a monastery near Rangoon.

Besant, Annie (1847–1933) Born Annie Wood, she married an Anglican clergyman, Frank Besant, but they separated due to doctrinal differences. She was a social reformer and secularist, crusading for freedom of thought, birth control, and women's rights. President of the Theosophical Society from 1907, after the death of Blavatsky in 1891 and Olcott in 1907, until her death in 1933. Besant popularised Theosophical teachings and built up the movement, spending much of her life in India, where she founded the Central Hindu College at Varanasi and was politically active for Indian independence.

besom A broom made of twigs, often birch, tied round a stick; the traditional witches' broomstick; the besom is used to clear the boundaries of the ritual space either symbolically (if indoors) or in actuality (if outdoors), and is leapt over by couples at handfastings since it is regarded as a symbol of male and female sexual union (the rod in the bush).

Beth, Rae Pagan author and hedgewitch, whose books include *Hedgewitch* (1990) and *Reincarnation and the Dark Goddess* (1994).

binah ('Understanding') The 3rd sephiroth or emanation in the Kabbalistic Tree of Life, Binah is situated at the head of the pillar of severity and makes up the supernal triangle along with Kether and Chokmah. It is the first feminine principle, the womb of the divine mother which receives the divine energy of Chokmah.

binding As part of the Wiccan ritual of initiation, initiates have their hands bound behind their backs with cords, and further cords around ankles and knees, as a symbol of the commitment being made to the coven and to Wicca. Binding spells can also be used to annul the effects of negative thoughts or actions.

Blavatsky, Helena Petrovna (1831–1891) Russian-born co-founder of the Theosophical Society, Blavatsky exhibited psychic powers from an early age and travelled widely in the East. With Henry Steel Olcott, she founded the Theosophical Society in America in 1875. Her writings include *Isis Unveiled* (1877) and *The Secret Doctrine* (1888).

'Blessed Be' Standard greeting among Wiccans and increasingly among Pagans. Its origins are unknown, but it is likely to have derived from Christian liturgical sayings such as 'Blessed Be the fruit of thy womb, Jesus'.

blindfold   As part of the initiation ritual of Wicca, initiates are blindfold as a mark of trust.

blood   Beliefs in the magical powers of blood are widespread world-wide. In Paganism, the power of women's menstrual blood is celebrated, and blood is sometimes taken from a thumb prick at initiation ceremonies to strengthen the bond between initiate and initiator.

blot, blotar   ('ceremony/ies; festival/s') Term used in Heathenism for ceremonies and celebrations. The Odinic Rite has set the blots down in an official form, with words for monthly celebrations, naming ceremonies, handfastings, funerals, and joining the Rite, in *The Book of Blots* (1991). The second Odinic Rite has produced *The Book of Blotar of the Odinic Rite*, which develops earlier versions found in the *Book of Blots* and does not expect practitioners to follow the rites as written but rather to evolve them.

body   The human body is celebrated as sacred rather than sinful in Paganism, particularly in Wicca where rituals are often performed naked, or 'skyclad'.

boline   A white-handled ritual knife used in Wicca for the preparation of incense or to cut things within a magical circle, or to cut a magical wand.

Bone, Eleanor 'Ray'   Wiccan High Priestess initiated by Gerald Gardner, who established a coven in south London. Along with Patricia Crowther and Monique Wilson, she was one of the three public faces of Gardnerian Wicca in the 1960s, giving interviews to newspapers and radio and television programmes. In 1966, the Oxford University Liberal Club chose her to replace the reigning Prime Minister, Harold Wilson, as an honorary member!

Book of Shadows   Wiccan book of invocations, rituals, information and lore which Gerald Gardner claimed had been copied by generations of initiates, but which was largely compiled by Gardner in the 1940s, borrowing from Crowley, Sir James Frazer, Celtic and Classical mythology, Rosicrucianism, Freemasonry, and Rudyard Kipling. It is extant as a manuscript, *Ye Bok of Ye Art Magical*, but has gone through many revisions as Wicca has grown and added to it or revised the material. It is copied by hand by each initiate into a particular tradition, and is often added to as experience is gained, so that no two books are exactly alike.

Alternatively, a personal Book of Shadows, or grimoire, is kept in which is written extra material gathered by the initiate. Computer 'disks of shadows' are often copied now that computer technology has permeated every aspect of life; however, in the UK at least these are often not a substitute for a hand-copied book but are an additional version. The Book of Shadows is traditionally kept secret, and only ever shown to a fellow initiate; as its name suggests, it is regarded as a shadowy reflection of the realities of the other world. The name may have been borrowed from Giordano Bruno's *De umbris idearum* of 1582, which itself may have derived from the *Liber de umbris* attributed to Solomon by the fourteenth century magician Cecco d'Ascoli.

Book of the Law   Also known as *Liber Al vel Legis*, the Book of the Law was written by Aleister Crowley in three days, supposedly dictated by his Holy Guardian Angel, Aiwass, in 1904. The book consists of a prose poem in three chapters, and announces the coming of a new age, the Aeon of Horus, which would overthrow all other religions. Crowley was to be its prophet. Its primary concept was complete self-fulfilment and the uniqueness of the individual, encapsulated in the Law of Thelema (the Greek word for 'will') and the saying, 'every man and woman is a star'. The Law of Thelema was a continuation of a theme which can be traced in Dee, Rabelais, and Nietszche, and states, 'do what thou wilt shall be the whole of the law', augmented with 'Love is the law; love under will'. The similarity of this law to the Wiccan Rede, 'An it harm none, do what thou wilt' indicates the influence of Crowley on the development of Wicca and Paganism and, indeed, Gardner met Crowley before the latter's death in 1947, and was made an honorary member of Crowley's O.·.T.·.O.·..

Bourne, Lois   High priestess of Gardner's Hertfordshire coven in the 1960s, but a solitary witch both preceding this time, and afterwards. She wrote two books, *Witch Amongst Us* (1989, with Colin Wilson) and *Dancing with Witches* (1998).

Bracelin, Jack L.   Friend of Gerald Gardner, who was credited with writing his biography, *Gerald Gardner, Witch* (1960), although in fact it was written by Idries Shah. Along with his girlfriend Dayonis, Bracelin led the pro-publicity faction of Gardner's coven and took over the running of the coven when Doreen Valiente's group seceded in 1957. They set up newspaper stories which led, in 1959, to adverse reports in *The People* and the coven going into hiding. The coven still exists today in North London. See also *Dayonis*.

Bride   Irish goddess of poetry, inspiration, healing and smithcraft, also known as Brighid, Brigit, or Brid. Since her festival day is 1st February, she is often celebrated at Imbolc rituals. See also *Candlemas; Imbolc.*

British Druid Order   One of the earliest, explicitly Pagan, druid orders to be founded in England (1979). The BDO has a shamanic and Wiccan influence, and is led by Joint Chiefs Philip Shallcrass and Emma Restall Orr ('Bobcat').

Brodie-Innes, J. W.   (1848–1923) Edinburgh lawyer, chief of the Amen Ra Temple of the Golden Dawn in that city until ejected by Mathers, and president of the Scottish Lodge of the Theosophical Society. In 1902, after Mathers was removed from office, Brodie-Innes along with Percy Bullock and R. W. Felkin headed the Golden Dawn, but an attempt to claim sole power which was foiled by A. E. Waite ultimately led to the demise of the Order. He subsequently joined the Stella Matutina and also became chief of the Alpha et Omega, both rival splinter groups of the defunct Golden Dawn.

Bruno, Giordano   (1548–1600) An apostate Dominican from Nola, near Naples, Giordano Bruno was a magician who believed that the Egyptian 'religion of the world' was purer than either Catholicism or Protestantism, although he sought for its return within a reformed Catholicism. This Egyptianism runs throughout Bruno's work, as he takes magic back to its pagan source rather than attempting to reconcile magic with Christianity. Bruno took the idea of divinity in nature and developed it into a 'nature religion' designed to replace the warring sects of Christians. This nature religion may have become a cult known as the Giordanisti, although there is no proof that this cult actually existed. Bruno portrayed the witch as transformer of society in *Cantus Circaeus* (1582) and *Spaccio della bestia trionfante* (1584), some three hundred years before Michelet's 1862 rendition of the same theme in *La Sorcière*. Bruno was burned at the stake in Rome on 17th February 1600, albeit as a heretic and magician, rather than as a witch.

Brythonic   Tradition which bases itself on religion as practised by the ancient Brythonic tribes who inhabited much of Wales, Scotland and England before being pushed to the far reaches of Wales, Scotland and Cornwall by the invading Romans in the years after 55 BCE. At this time, the Brythons also invaded Armorica (Brittany, in North Western France) and established themselves there. Followers of the modern Brythonic tradition draw inspiration from Keltic Welsh legends related in such writings as *The Mabinogion*, *The Red Book of Hergest*, and *The Black Book of Camarthen*, reviving the traditions outlined in these texts. Brythons live as a family based group, and instead of initiating newcomers, they are adopted into the family through an adoption ritual. The Brythonic tradition is dedicated to the Lady and Lord of this land of Britain, and deity names are those of the Brythonic/Welsh heritage, for example the goddesses Ceridwen and Rhiannon.

Buckland, Ray   One-time Gardnerian High Priest who emigrated to the USA in 1967, taking Gardnerian Wicca with him. He later became disillusioned with the perceived hierarchy in Gardnerian Wicca and went on to form a more egalitarian tradition of Wicca which he called Seax, or Saxon Wica *[sic]*. He is the author of several DIY guides to Wicca, including *The Tree: Complete Book of Saxon Witchcraft* (1974).

Budapest, Zsuzsanna   Hungarian-born feminist activist in the USA who was one of the prime movers behind the development of feminist witchcraft, forming the women-only Susan B. Anthony Coven, running a shop called The Feminist Wicca in California and self-publishing *The Feminist Book of Light and Shadows*. The book was a reworking of available Gardnerian witchcraft which excluded all mention of men and male deity and included her own rituals, spells and lore. It was later expanded and published as *The Holy Book of Women's Mysteries* in 1986. See also *Susan B. Anthony Coven*.

'Burning Times'   A phrase referring to the Great Witch Hunt of early modern Europe, commonly used in the USA but less so in England, where witches were hanged rather than burned.

C

Cabot, Laurie   American witch based in Salem, Massachusetts, and known as the 'official witch of Salem'. She is the founder of the Witches League for Public Awareness, which protested against the portrayal of witches in films such as *The Witches of Eastwick* (1987), and author of *Power of the Witch* (1990) and *The Witch in Every Woman* (1997).

Caduceus   Sacred to Mercury/Hermes, the caduceus is a wand with two serpents twined round it, surmounted by two small wings or a winged helmet, representing the story in which Mercury intervened in a fight between two serpents whereupon they curled themselves round his wand. For the Romans the caduceus served as a symbol of moral equilibrium and good conduct – the wand represents power, the two snakes, wisdom, the wings diligence and the helmet lofty thoughts. The caduceus also signified the integration of the four elements, the wand being earth, the wings air, the serpents fire and water. As the staff of the god of healing, the caduceus has been appropriated by the medical profession

Cakes and Wine   Sacred meal, consisting of consecrated cakes and wine, taken at the end of a ritual. In some traditions, such as Wicca, the consecration of cakes and wine can be quite elaborate, borrowing from high ceremonial magic and using words written by Aleister Crowley. The wine is charged with energy by lowering the point of the athame into the chalice of wine, thus symbolising the union of male and female in the symbolic Great Rite. The cakes are also charged with an earth-invoking pentagram drawn over them with the athame. In other traditions, the cakes and wine (or cakes and ale) are blessed in a more simple manner before they are shared by all participants. Cakes can as often be bread or biscuits; wine or ale can as often be a non-alcoholic drink.

candle   Candles are used to a great extent in Pagan ritual, with candlelight operating as one of many mechanisms which allow the movement from everyday reality to an altered state of consciousness. Colours of candles are often chosen to reflect the purpose of the particular rite (gold for Midsummer; white/silver for a full moon, for example), as is their number in more ceremonial groups. Candles are also used for candle magic, where magical intent is poured into the candle, perhaps as an essential oil with the right associations for the purpose is slowly rubbed into it; the candle is then burned.

Candlemas   One of the eight festivals which make up the Wheel of the Year, Candlemas is celebrated on or around 2nd February, and is actually a Christian festival. In modern Paganism, it has become confused with the Gaelic Imbolc/Imbolg, or Bride's Day (31st January/1st February). Since most Pagan groups gather at a time which suits their members, usually the nearest Friday or Saturday to a festival date, the dates for Candlemas and Imbolc could easily have become conflated, and with the Celticisation of Paganism and its festivals, few outside Wicca now refer to this festival as Candlemas.

Carmina Gaedelica A collection of songs, poems and tales gathered by Alexander Carmichael (1832–1912) in the Scottish highlands over the course of many years working for the Excise service. The title is Latin for 'Gaelic hymns/songs/incantations' which were gathered in six volumes, two of which were published in 1900 and the remaining four of which were completed by his daughter and grandson after his death. The *Carmina Gaedelica* is used as a source book for rituals by some Pagans, particularly Druids.

Cardell, Charles (d.1976) English psychologist and self-proclaimed Wiccan who published a Gardnerian Book of Shadows under the pseudonym Rex Nemorensis once Gardner died in 1964. His material came from Olive Greene, who had turned against Gardner and passed details to Cardell, although there is some suggestion that she was Cardell's agent all along.

Carr-Gomm, Philip Chosen Chief of the Order of Bards, Ovates and Druids, who re-founded the order in February 1988.

cauldron One of the key features of witchcraft in the popular imagination, along with broomsticks and black cats. The cauldron is in fact a large cooking pot, and has a long tradition back to ancient times. In Greek myth, for example, the high priestess of Hecate, Medea, is described brewing magical potions in her cauldron by Ovid, whilst magic cauldrons feature in British and Irish mythology (for example, the Dagda's cauldron of rejuvenation and inspiration, and Ceridwen's cauldron of inspiration, from which emerged the three drops of Wisdom, the mystical Awen of the Druids). Cauldrons dating back to the late Bronze Age have been discovered in archaeological digs, the most famous being the solid silver Gundestrap Cauldron found in Jutland, which is embellished with scenes from mythology. The cauldron is, of course, a predominant feature of the witch image in Shakespeare's *Macbeth* (1606). In modern witchcraft, the cauldron is a symbol of nature and the uterus of the Great Mother Goddess, the cauldron of regeneration in which all things are transformed; but rather than brewing potions in it, the cauldron is now predominantly used for scrying (when it is filled with water and black ink) or for fires (when methylated spirit or alcohol is lit within the cauldron and the fire danced around and leapt over).

Celts Term established in the eighteenth and nineteenth centuries to refer to prehistoric and early historic peoples of Europe who, divided into tribal groupings, inhabited the British Isles from the Bronze Age until at least the fifth century BCE. The Celts were conquered by the invading Romans after 43 CE, leaving only Ireland untouched. The history of the Celts before their contact with the Roman Empire is particularly obscure, and their religion hard to interpret. Archaeological findings abound, and there is a wealth of conjectural literature in Greek, Roman and Irish sources, but nothing definitive has emerged. It would appear that the Celts believed in life after death, since archaeology has revealed graves filled with carefully chosen grave goods, and Caesar wrote that the Gauls believed in transmigration of souls and believed themselves to be descended from the god of the underworld. Archaeological evidence also suggests that the Celts had established trade links with the Etruscans, Greeks and Romans as early as the third century BCE. Classical sources report that, around 500 BCE the Celts took Spain from the Carthaginians, and a century later conquered Northern Italy at the expense of the Etruscans, and settled in large numbers in Gaul (Brittany). It seems highly unlikely that such a disparate group of people would have shared the same culture and religious beliefs and practices, and indeed, some have argued that there is no such thing as a 'Celtic race' – the term 'Keltoi', according to some, was used to mean simply 'foreigners' rather than to denote a specific ethnic group.

The Druidic priesthood was believed to be the sovereign power in Celtic society, according to classical sources, and it is from these sources that the association of Druids with mistletoe, oak, golden sickles, sacred groves, esoteric learning, and human sacrifice derives. Although little is known of ancient Druidry, nevertheless many Pagans draw on stories about Druidry, and on Celtic deities, sacred places, and calendars for spiritual inspiration, as do some Christians and New Age practitioners. The descendants of the Celts are popularly regarded as Scots, Irish, Welsh, Breton, Manx, Northumbrian, Cornish and West Country people, but for many who draw on things Celtic for spiritual purposes, everyone can claim to be Celtic, in terms of culture if not ethnicity.

After the Roman occupation, a revival of Celtic art and culture occurred and Celtic Christianity grew more vigorous. However, the Celtic peoples were largely conquered, absorbed and assimilated into English culture, although the Celtic languages survived, aided by the nationalistic Celtic revival of the eighteenth century.

Celtic Revival   Term used to describe the rediscovery of and fascination with the Celtic past in the eighteenth and nineteenth centuries, which included the revival of Gaelic language and poetry, poetry and cultural festivals such as the Eisteddfodau, traditional forms of dress, and the study and publication of ancient texts and stories. The revival was largely associated with the growth of nationalism and the independence movement in Ireland, but was also important for Scottish and Welsh nationalism.

Celticisation   Process by which Wicca and Paganism have become increasingly Celtic, particularly in names of seasonal festivals where Candlemas became Imbolc, Lammas became Lughnasadh (though remained interchangeable), Autumn Equinox Mabon, and Hallowe'en Samhain. This came about largely as a result of two processes: the increasing influence of United States Paganism in Britain, and the move to Ireland of the prolific Pagan authors Janet and Stewart Farrar. The trend now seems to have reached its high point, and many Pagans use different names interchangeably.

censer   Vessel in which incense is burned during rituals, also known as a thurible.

ceremonial magic   Systems of magic deriving chiefly from the Jewish and Christian kabbalahs during the Renaissance, originally practised by educated men, including priests and doctors. It can thus be strongly religious in character, and seeks to control the powers of nature, characterised as either angelic or demonic, through the use of powerful divine names such as Agla, Adonai, and Tetragrammaton (from the Jewish kabbalah). The systems are usually complicated and call for a great deal of purification and consecration of both magician, ritual space, and magical tools. Once a solitary practice, contemporary ceremonial magicians often meet together in groups or Lodges made up of both men and women, as well as working alone.

Ceridwen   Mother Goddess of Welsh origin who prepares the cauldron of wisdom and inspiration with a brew made from six plants. Whilst looking after it, Gwion accidentally drank three drops when he splashed his hand, and thus became possessed of all knowledge. Ceridwen pursued Gwion through many changes (a greyhound chasing a hare, an otter chasing a fish, a hawk chasing a bird) before eating him whilst she was a hen and he a grain of corn. She then gave birth to him as Taliesin, greatest of the Welsh bards. Her symbol is a great white sow, and she is venerated as a dark goddess.

Cernunnos   Celtic deity known only from a name inscribed in a Gaulish altar. He is believed to be an embodiment of stags, whose antlers represent the spirit of the forest. Cernunnos is a major god form in Wicca, where he is regarded as a fertility and chthonic deity, consort of the goddess, and is generally called the 'Hornèd God', or 'Hornèd One'. He is perceived in a variety of aspects throughout the Wheel of the Year.

chakra ('wheel') Energy centres in the human body, typically seven in number but sometimes more, which begin at the base of the spine and ascend up the spine to the crown of the head. Each chakra is perceived as a coloured, spinning light, the colours following those of the spectrum (red at the base, purple at the third eye, white at the crown). The concept of chakras and the practice of opening them in order to channel energy has been borrowed from Hindu tantra via Theosophy, and is used by Wiccans and magicians.

Chaldean Chronicles Chronicles written by and about the inhabitants of the ancient country of Chaldea which formed part of Babylonia, in what is now southern Iraq.

chalice Linked to the symbolism of the cauldron, the chalice represents the female regenerative powers, the womb of the Mother Goddess, and is joined with the male symbol of the athame in the ceremony of cakes and wine – the union of the male with the female consecrates the wine which is to be shared. The chalice has obvious links with other religions, including Christianity, and to the Holy Grail of Arthurian legend.

challenge The point in the Wiccan initiation ceremony when the initiate is met with the point of a ritual sword against his or her chest and challenged to enter the circle if the initiate has the courage to pass from the world of men into the realm of the Lords of the Outer Spaces. If the challenge is accepted, the initiate is allowed to pass through the gateway and into the Wiccan circle as part of the symbolic rebirth into Wicca.

chant The regular rhythm of chants is used for a variety of purposes in Pagan groups – as a means of entering a trance state for ritual working, to work magic, to invoke a deity or, simply, as a means of relaxing and enjoyment after a ritual has ended.

chaos The primeval void which existed before the formation of the universe, Chaos was the first thing which came into being, according to the Greek creation myth. From it were born Nyx (night) and Erebus (darkness) which then gave birth to Aether (brightness) and Hemera (day). Alternatively, Chaos was the offspring of the Titan Kronos.

Chaos Magic   An occult tradition which began in England in the late 1970s, drawing on scientific chaos theory. Austin Osman Spare (1888–1956) is claimed as its founder, but the fundamental principles of Chaos Magic did not appear until Peter Carroll's *Liber Null* and *Psychonaut* were published in 1978, followed by Ray Sherwin's *The Book of Results* (1978). Along with mathematician Charles Brewster, Carroll and Sherwin decided that chaos theory held the secret to how magic really works. Chaos magic incorporates Spare's sigil magic and uses a basic formula for opening and closing circles drawn from the German Fraternatis Saturnii, embellished with concepts drawn from fiction. It argues against dogmatism, has few core principles, and favours contradiction and flexibility. The emphasis is on doing rather than theorising, and personal experience, coupled with rigorous self-assessment and analysis, is paramount. An eclectic approach to magic is thus encouraged, and the chaos magician's only aim is to detach from the established web of notions about self, society and the world.

charge   words spoken during a ritual by a person on whom deity has been invoked, and who is therefore regarded as the embodiment of a particular goddess or god for the duration of that ritual. It may contain commands or instructions to the coven.

Charge of the Goddess   The name given to a charge written by Doreen Valiente for Gerald Gardner's Book of Shadows, drawn from Aleister Crowley who in turn drew on Charles Leland's *Aradia, or the Gospel of the Witches* for his inspiration. It is perhaps the only text which could be called liturgical in Wicca, and contains instructions for ritual, the blessings of the Goddess, the nature of divinity, and the relationship between Wicca and the divine.

charms   A means of healing and protecting, employed by cunning men and women as well as magicians, which were often written on a scrap of paper which the sufferer would then wear. Charms are frequently corruptions of Christian prayers, particularly Latin ones, but they can often be traced back from the Medieval period to Classical Greek and Roman religion or to the Anglo-Saxon period.

chesed   ('mercy') The fourth sephira on the kabbalistic Tree of Life, which brings the vision of love. Its symbols are the tetrahedron, pyramid and equal-armed cross, and its image is a crowned and throned king. It is also called 'Gedullah' ('greatness').

chokmah ('wisdom') The second sephira on the kabbalistic Tree of Life. Chokmah brings the vision of God face to face. Its symbols are the lingam and phallus, the standing stone, tower and straight line. It is known as the Crown of Creation, the point at which God enters the world, and is situated at the head of the Pillar of Mercy.

chthonic Relating to or inhabiting the underworld.

Church of All Worlds (CAW) Organisation founded in 1962 by two students from Westminster College, Missouri (Oberon Zell and Lance Christie and their wives) using science fiction as religious literature. Its central ideas are taken from Robert Heinlein's novel *Stranger in a Strange Land* (1962), which tells the story of Valentine Michael Smith, born of Earth parents but raised on Mars by aliens, who returns to Earth as an alien and eventually creates a religion, the Church of All Worlds. The Church of All Worlds, both in the novel and in actuality, forms communities called 'nests' and now describes itself as a Neo-Pagan religion 'dedicated to the celebration of Life, the maximal actualization of Human potential, and the realisation of ultimate individual freedom and personal responsibility in harmonious eco-psychic relationship with the total Biosphere of Holy Mother Earth' (CAW's statement of purpose). The central idea of the Church is 'Thou Art God'. In 1971 the CAW became the first Pagan organisation to win federal tax-exempt status. It publishes *Green Egg* magazine four times a year.

Circe A powerful enchantress in Greek mythology who turned men into animals. Daughter of Helios (the sun god) and Perse (an oceanid), Circe lived on the island of Aeaea, where she detained Odysseus for a year on his return from Troy to Ithaca. She is the aunt of Medea, and both are priestesses of Hecate. Allegorised to represent brute pleasure which turns men into animals, Circe is regarded in Wicca as a witch, priestess and goddess who represents the power of transformation and holds within her the secrets of regeneration.

circle The circle is a magical space delineated by tracing the shape in the air with sword or athame and, sometimes, drawn in chalk on the floor. The casting of the circle symbolically removes the participants from the reality of the ordinary, everyday world ('the world of men') into a neutral space in which the Gods can be approached. In Wicca, it is thus spoken of as 'a boundary between the world of men and the realms of the Mighty Ones'.

The circle can also be a synonym for a coven or larger gathering of Wiccans, or for a ritual.

Circle Sanctuary First established by Selena Fox and Jim Alan as Church of Circle Wicca in 1974 in Wisconsin, USA, the purchase of land in 1983 led to the renaming of the group as Circle Sanctuary, now a legal church. Circle sponsors many sabbats and festivals, including the Pagan Spirit Gathering (PSG) each Midsummer and the Pagan Unity Festival at Autumn Equinox. Circle produces *Circle Network News* a major communication channel for Pagans in the US, and is still run by Selena, with her second husband, Dennis Carpenter.

Clan of Tubal-Cain Name of Robert Cochrane's coven. Cochrane had worked as a blacksmith for a time, and named his coven after the great smith from Hebrew legend.

Clutterbuck, Dorothy (1880–1951) Dorothy Clutterbuck was said to have initiated Gerald Gardner into her New Forest coven in 1939. 'Old Dorothy' was a teacher of music and elocution, and closely involved with the Co-Masonic Rosicrucian Theatre in Christchurch, Hampshire which she had helped to found and which allegedly harboured an inner circle of hereditary witches, of which she was the leader. Not a great deal is known about her, though her father was a captain in the Indian Army 14th Sikhs, her upbringing was amongst the British Raj in India, and her married name was Fordham. Gardner described her as an elegant, graceful lady with dark, wavy hair, and referred to her in various publications, publishing the rituals of her coven in fictional form in *High Magic's Aid* (1949). It was for a time believed that she did not exist and Gardner had invented her, but through the research of Doreen Valiente and, later, Ronald Hutton, it seems that she was in fact a pillar of the establishment in the Highcliffe area, and had no known connections with either the Rosicrucian Theatre or with witchcraft. Hutton suggests that Gardner used her to divert attention from Dafo, the woman with whom he worked who really was a witch priestess.

CoBDO See *Council of British Druid Orders*.

Cochrane, Robert (1936–1966) (born Roy Bowers) Founder of a style of witchcraft significantly different from Gardner's in the early 1960s. Cochrane claimed to be a hereditary witch descended from a coven in Warwickshire through which he traced his ancestry to 1724. He claimed to have been initiated at the age of five, by either his mother or a male relative, and also claimed that two of his ancestors had been hanged for witchcraft. He became Magister, or head of his coven aged twenty-eight, and having worked for a time as a blacksmith, he named this coven the Clan of Tubal-Cain, after the great smith from Hebrew legend. Doreen Valiente was initiated into his Sussex-based coven in 1964, and she suggests that Cochrane and Gardner were both mischievous, devious, and had a penchant for fabrication. Cochrane, however, hated the Gardnerian craft and believed his tradition to be more genuine. Doreen Valiente thinks that Cochrane actually coined the phrase 'Gardnerian Wicca' as a term of abuse, despite the fact that his rituals were very similar to those of Gardner except for the tradition of working in black robes instead of skyclad, working out of doors, absence of the scourge, and different correspondences for the elements (fire in the east, earth in the south, water in the west, and air in the north). Cochrane also led the coven as Magister, whilst Gardner's covens were led by High Priestesses. Polemics between the two groups surfaced in the *Pentagram*, the official journal of the Witchcraft Research Association, in 1965, leading to the folding of both the journal and the association in 1966. At this point, Valiente left Cochrane's group, having become disillusioned by his fabrications and annoyed by his attacks on Gardnerian witches. After becoming obsessed with hallucinogenic drugs, including fly agaric (*amanita muscaria*) and deadly nightshade (*atropa belladonna*), Cochrane died at the Midsummer Solstice in 1966, allegedly committing suicide through an overdose of narcotic herbs and barbiturates. Before his death, however, Cochrane was in contact with Joseph Wilson in the USA, which led to the founding in North America of the 1734 tradition, and later the Roebuck. A significant British group known as the Regency was also founded by several of Cochrane's friends. See also *Jones, Evan John; Owen, Ruth Wynn; Plant Brân; Regency; 1734.*

Corn King Harvest aspect of the Horned God, drawing on the old folk song John Barleycorn and the mummers' plays in which his role was played by a mummer dressed in tufts of corn. He becomes king at Midsummer (June 21st) but his reign is short as he is sacrificed by the Goddess at Lammas (August 1st).

collective unconscious A term borrowed from Jungian psychology and used in some Wiccan groups. The collective unconscious is the part of the unconscious mind derived from ancestral memory and experience common to all humankind, and is thus distinct from the personal unconscious. For some Wiccans it is thus believed to be the realm in which the gods exist.

colours   An integrative part of the chain of associations which make up correspondences. Different colours have particular associations with, for instance, chakras, sephiroth, planets, elements etc. which are consciously built up and used in magic.

Co-Masonry   The Order of International Co-Freemasonry, generally known as Co-Masonry, began in France in 1882 when a French masonic lodge decided to initiate a woman and was thus expelled by their governing body. As a result, they began their own Masonic order which admitted women and men on equal terms, unlike Freemasonry. Annie Besant was initiated in 1902 and enthusiastically spread Co-Masonry in England and the English-speaking world of Theosophy. After her death, it was led by her daughter, Mabel Besant-Scott. Co-Masonry still exists and has its headquarters in Paris. Membership is through initiation, elevation is through degrees, and a mixture of philosophy, religion and ritual is taught, while its members help each other in material matters. It was the Fellowship of Crotona, an occult group of Co-Masons established by Mabel Besant-Scott, which allegedly contained the hidden inner group of hereditary witches who initiated Gardner in 1939.

cone of power   Energy raised by a coven in a meeting is shaped by willpower into a cone. The cone is raised normally by members linking hands and dancing in the circle whilst chanting the Witches' Rune. Once raised, the energy is available for use throughout the ritual.

consciousness raising   A feminist practice which allows for the exploration of women's preconscious wishes and desires outside of psychoanalysis.

consecration   In order to purify articles for use in magic, they are often consecrated by being passed through the four elements of earth (earth or pentacle), air (incense smoke), fire (candle flame) and water and then energised between the bodies of two people, usually male and female. They are then blessed, and are ready for use.

cords   Cords of varying colours, each measuring nine feet in length, are an integral part of Wiccan initiation rituals, where the initiate is bound with them to symbolise the commitment made between the coven, initiator and new initiate – almost like an umbilical cord. They are linked to the element of earth, and thus act as a reminder that the initiate is still bound to the essential material place even though she or he has stepped into the realm of magic and spirit. Cords are also used in magic – in the Witches' Ladder, where knots are tied in the cord, in wheels which are formed by a coven linking their cords to form the shape of a wheel, and in bindings.

Corpus Hermeticum A body of magical and philosophical texts attributed to Hermes Trismegistus, said to originate on an emerald tablet inscribed by the Egyptian god Thoth (Hermes Trismegistus in the Græco-Roman tradition). The manuscripts were thought to date from vast antiquity, long before Plato and even longer before Christ – indeed, Hermes Trismegistus was believed by some to be a contemporary of Moses, and by others to have lived at the same time as Noah. The corpus was, however, misdated and it is now known that the writings were by various authors and of varying dates. Isaac Casaubon, in 1614, is generally regarded as the first person to disprove the pre-Christian provenance of the Hermetic manuscripts. In the late fifteenth century, these manuscripts, containing elements of Platonism, Neo-platonism, Stoicism, neo-Pytha-goreanism, and Jewish and Persian influences, were brought to Cosimo de Medici in Florence. Marsilio Ficino (1433–99), a physician and scholar, was immediately instructed to begin their translation. With a strong emphasis on astrological and alchemical lore, the teachings of the corpus claimed that, through the power of mystical regeneration, it is possible for humankind to regain the supremacy over nature that was lost at the time of the Biblical Fall. The Hermetic tradition is still widely recognised and adopted by modern occultists practising intellectual magic.

correspondences Systems of magical correspondences, both real and symbolic, are believed in magic to exist throughout all parts of the universe, both visible and invisible, forming associative clusters of phenomena thought to share common affinities, the purpose of which is to link the microcosm with the macrocosm. For example, the kabbalistic sephira of Yesod is associated with such things as: the Moon (planet), violet (colour), 9 (number), quartz (precious stone), mandrake (plant), jasmine (perfume). These are in turn associated with other phenomena: thus, the Moon relates to specific lunar deities such as Diana/Artemis, Selene, Hecate, Thoth, Ashtarte, and to water (the element which it rules), mirrors (due to its reflective nature), the sea, tides and flux, the colour silver as well as violet, moonstone as well as quartz. In this way, huge systems of magical correspondences are built up such that the mention of 'Yesod' or 'the Moon' automatically sets off a chain of images, linked through association, which can be used in magical ritual.

Council of British Druid Orders (CoBDO)   An organisation representing different Druid orders, founded in 1988 in response to problems at the Stonehenge summer solstice celebrations of that year.

coven   A group of witches who have been initiated into a tradition of Wicca or witchcraft and meet regularly for religious festivals and for training. The word may derive from the French 'couvent' and the Latin 'conventus', meaning 'gathering' or 'meeting', but there is no evidence that coven was associated with witchcraft prior to the 1930s. Gardner wrote that a coven should consist of thirteen people – six men, six women, and a leader – but although thirteen is often cited as the upper limit for coven numbers, the number of members might be considerably lower – five or six individuals, or even fewer.

Covenant of the Goddess (COG)   North American association which constitutes a loose association of Pagan groups. COG was founded at Midsummer in 1975 in an attempt to forge an alliance between various Wiccan groups as a response to harassment and persecution. Its principles state an intent to secure for witches and covens the legal protection enjoyed by members of other religions. COG was incorporated as a religious organisation in California at Hallowe'en 1975, and is a legally registered church; however, its charter includes respect for the anarchic nature of the Craft and does not dictate belief, policy or practice.

covenstead   The meeting place of a coven, which may be a fixed and regularly used room or an outdoor site.

Craft   An alternative name for Wicca or witchcraft. However, 'the Craft' is also used to denote Freemasonry and, increasingly, Druidry and is thus very unspecific.

creation   In Paganism, the creation of the world is largely regarded as natural and female, creation is 'born' rather than 'made' mechanically.

crone   In Wicca and some forms of Paganism, the goddess is seen as triform, appearing as maiden, mother and crone. The triple goddess was promulgated by Jane Ellen Harrison in the early twentieth century, but is perhaps best known among Pagans from Robert Graves' *The White Goddess* (1948). The crone represents the wise woman, the hag, who carries with her the wisdom of life and experience.

cross quarter days A name given to the festivals held between the solstices and equinoxes – Imbolc, Beltane, Lammas and Samhain – also known as the Greater Sabbats and as the Celtic Fire Festivals.

Crowley, Aleister (1875–1947) Crowley was initiated into the London temple of the Golden Dawn in November 1898 at the age of 23, and initially used the Order as a launching pad for his invectives against Christianity, for which he had a hatred which stemmed from his Plymouth Brethren upbringing. He expressed his 'agreement with Shelley and Nietzsche in defining Christianity as the religious expression of the slave spirit in man' in the preface to his poem *The World's Tragedy* (1910: XXIX). His natural aptitude for magic paved his meteoric rise through the grades. Although at first close to Mathers, he became intensely competitive with the Chief and was subsequently expelled from the Order. Confident of his own abilities, however, Crowley awarded himself the highest grade of Ipsissimus, and went on to found the Argenteum Astrum (A∴A∴), or Order of the Silver Star, through whose journal *The Equinox* he published many of the Golden Dawn's secret rituals between 1909 and 1913. In 1912, Crowley became involved in the Ordo Templi Orientis (O∴T∴O∴), a German system of occultism, becoming the head of the Order in 1922. In 1920 he founded his Abbey of Thelema in Sicily, which he envisioned as a magical colony from which to launch the new aeon, the Age of Horus, of which Crowley considered himself to be the chosen prophet. However, the new aeon seemed not to be destined to begin in Sicily after all, as Crowley was expelled by Mussolini in 1923. Crowley's Thelema was propagated through his Argenteum Astrum and his prolific writings, the most important of which is his *Book of the Law.*

The influence of Crowley on Wicca, despite Gardner's refutations to the contrary, is clear. Crowley's work appears in Wiccan ritual, and Doreen Valiente has openly stated that she rewrote much of Gardner's material, replacing that which was obviously Crowley's with her own poetry. Crowley's Law of Thelema is an obvious influence on Gardner's Wiccan Rede, and his wording for the blessing of the cakes in the Gnostic Mass – 'Lord most secret, bless this spiritual food unto our bodies, bestowing upon us health and wealth and strength and joy and peace, and that fulfilment of will and of love under will that is perpetual happiness' – is almost identical to that used in Wicca: 'O Queen most secret, bless this food unto our bodies, bestowing health, wealth, strength, joy and peace, and that fulfilment of love which is perpetual happiness'. Crowley's invocation 'by seed and root and stem and bud and leaf and flower' has been incorporated verbatim into Gardner's Book of Shadows, and Valiente's 'Charge of the Goddess', which is perhaps the only liturgical text commonly used in Wicca, was rewritten from an earlier Charge from Crowley's Gnostic Mass, which he in turn took from Leland. Further influences on Paganism come mainly through Crowley's continuation of the Golden Dawn system, in terms of using goddesses as well as gods, allowing men and women equal access to his order and further systematising magical lore. Additionally, Crowley's fascination with the East and his accomplished practice of yoga along with his mentor, Allan Bennett, infused his basic Golden Dawn-derived system with practices and terms drawn from Eastern philosophies, such as karma, chakras, kundalini, tantra, yoga, reincarnation, mantras and prana. Thus, Crowley consciously integrated Eastern philosophies and practices with the western esoteric and magical theories which formed the foundation of his Thelema.

Crowley, Vivianne Wiccan Priestess, psychologist and university lecturer, Vivianne Crowley was initiated into both Alexandrian and Gardnerian Wicca, and in 1979 founded a Wiccan coven which combined the two traditions. In 1988, she founded the Wicca Study Group along with her husband, Chris, and it is now Europe's largest Wiccan teaching organisation. She is a member of the Pagan Federation council, serving as Honorary Secretary (1988–94), Prison Chaplaincy Co-ordinator (1991–5), and Interfaith Co-ordinator (1994–6). Crowley has a doctorate in psychology and has trained in transpersonal counselling with the Centre for Transpersonal Psychology in London. Her books include the best-selling *Wicca: the Old Religion in the New Millennium* (1989; 1996), *Phoenix From the Flame: Pagan Spirituality in the Western World* (1994), *Principles of Paganism* (1996), *Principles of Wicca* (1997), *Principles of Jungian Spirituality* (1998), *A Woman's Kabbalah* (2000), *Ancient Wisdom* (2000), *Carl Jung: Journey of Transformation* (2000), *Your Dark Side* (2001), *Magic and Mysteries of Ancient Egypt* (2001) and *A Woman's Guide to the Earth Traditions* (2001).

Crowther, Pat (b. 1932) Gardnerian High Priestess, initiated by Gerald Gardner in 1960, who established covens in Yorkshire and Lancashire. She was an actress and dancer whose husband Arnold Crowther, whom she married in 1960 and initiated soon after her own initiation, was a magician in the theatre. He was an old friend of Gerald Gardner, and introduced Patricia to him as well as introducing Gardner to Aleister Crowley. Arnold died of a heart attack on 1st May 1974, having been ill for some time.

Some years later, in May 1981, she was handfasted to Ian Lilleyman, with whom she still runs a coven in Sheffield. Patricia Crowther is the author of a number of books on witchcraft, including *Lid Off the Cauldron* (1981) and her autobiography *One Witch's World* (1998), published as *High Priestess: The Life and Times of Patricia Crowther* (2000) in the USA. An ex-member of her coven, Pat Kopanski, was instrumental in getting Alex Sanders initiated into Wicca.

cunning person   A term used during the medieval period to denote a white witch, or practitioner of beneficial magic, thus distinguishing them from maleficent witches. In fact, they claimed to be able to counteract magic and spells cast by witches, and to identify witches, as well as offering herbal healing to local people, finding lost property and detecting thieves. The cunning man learned his profession from his parents, and often claimed a long tradition back through generations.

cup   See *chalice*.

curses   Traditionally cast by witches, curses are intended to cause harm, illness or death. Despite claims that cursing is not part of contemporary Wicca or Paganism, it is still generally acknowledged that those who can heal can also harm!

D

Dafo   Music and elocution teacher, and witch priestess, who lived near Christchurch, Hampshire and worked with Gerald Gardner before Wicca was publicised. She was a close friend of Gardner throughout the 1940s, and leading lady and stage director of the Rosicrucian Theatre. In 1947, Gardner and Dafo formed the Ancient Crafts Ltd, a company used to buy a plot of land adjacent to the naturist club at St Albans to which Gardner belonged. On this land, the company erected a reconstruction of a sixteenth century witch's cottage, obtained from the Abbey Folklore Museum at New Barnet which had closed in 1945. A coven led by Dafo and Gardner flourished in the cottage in the early 1950s, but Dafo withdrew at the close of 1952 due to ill health and in order to escape Gardner's publicising activities with her reputation intact.

Dagda   The 'good god' of the Tuatha Dé Danann in Celtic mythology, after whose daughters (Eire, Banbha and Fodhla) Ireland was named.

Daly, Mary   American radical feminist writer who played a leading role in inserting witchcraft into feminism in the mid-1970s by claiming that the Great Witch Hunt represented the control of women and the Old Religion, albeit with an emphasis on witchcraft as an obstacle to patriarchy rather than as a religion. She urged women to reclaim their power by identifying with the witches, using the myth of nine million as a testament to the terrors of patriarchal and Christian persecution, and relying heavily on Margaret Murray for a reconstruction of witchcraft in the early modern period.

dance   One of the eight paths of magic in Wicca, dance is used within Paganism to enter a trance state, to raise energy for ritual and spells, and simply to express joy. The spiral dance, for example, echoes the spirals of life and describes the cone of power created by the dance as female and male dancers link hands alternately, progressing in a ring until the leader of the dance leads them off into a spiral. Power is raised for ritual and spells by dancing in a circle, often with a chant, until energy is raised; sometimes, this type of dance may be performed around a person in need of magical help, or around a tree, fire or standing stone. This dance appears to operate as a bridging mechanism between the formalised framework of the ritual construction of sacred space and the inner sanctum, where the initiates meet with the divine, and its rhythms bind the group together.

Dark Goddess   An aspect of the Triple Goddess often known as the Hag or Crone, associated with death, wisdom, transformation and the underworld. She takes the Corn King in sacrifice at Lammas, opening the way for his descent into the Underworld at Autumn Equinox where she joins him as Queen of the Underworld at Hallowe'en.

dark moon   The fourth phase of the moon, when the moon has waned to nothing and the new moon is still three days away. At this time, the moon cannot be seen in the night sky, and it is regarded as a time for baleful magic.

Dayonis   Girlfriend of Jack Bracelin, who led the pro-publicity faction of Gardner's coven and took over the running of the coven after the secession of Doreen Valiente's group in 1957. In newspaper and magazine articles, Dayonis claimed to have been brought up in a Pagan witch family.

death   In Wicca and Paganism, death is regarded as a rite of passage in which the physical body is shed. To some, the liberated spirit then travels to the Summerlands, Caer Arianrhod, or other such place, where it rests until the time comes for rebirth in a new human body. To others, who do not believe in reincarnation, the spirit may rest eternal. In whatever way the spirit is perceived to journey, death is regarded as an essential part of the natural cycle, mirroring the seasonal cycles of nature reflected in the Wheel of the Year.

Dee, John   (1527–1608) Elizabethan astrologer, alchemist and magician, and confidant of Elizabeth I, Dee was regarded as something of a cunning man. He travelled widely and built up an extensive library on magic in England and in Europe. He collaborated with Edward Kelly in scrying and seances, and they developed the angelic Enochian language with which to communicate with angels and perform Enochian magic. Under James I, Dee lost his royal patronage, and died in poverty at his home, Mortlake, in Surrey.

degrees   Levels of initiation in Wicca, based on knowledge and experience, deriving from Masonic rituals of advancement. Criticised by some as hierarchical, degrees of initiation are regarded as a measure of experience and ability attained by individual initiates. However, no standard or benchmark exists against which initiates can be measured before they are given a further degree. Rather, a candidate's readiness for a further initiation is judged by the initiating High Priestess or High Priest, often in consultation with her or his partner, and after discussion with the initiate. Covens usually consist of first and second degree initiates, and perhaps some third degrees. It is usual, however, for third degrees to leave the parent coven to form their own group or work with a partner, and it is becoming increasingly common for second degree couples to also 'hive off' and start their own coven, though under the guidance of the parent coven rather than as fully independent. Some forms of Druidry also practice initiation, as do nearly all magical and occult organisations. See also *first degree; initiation; second degree; third degree.*

deity   Gods and goddesses who, in Paganism, can originate from a variety of different pantheons.

Demeter   Greek corn goddess whose daughter, Persephone, was abducted by Hades and became Queen of the Underworld. She was associated with both death and corn, for in Athens the dead were called *demeteroi* and corn was traditionally scattered on new graves. Her cult was one of the mystery cults of the ancient world, with entry by initiation and veiled in secrecy. The most famous cult centre was at Eleusis, where the Eleusinian Mysteries were celebrated. See also *Eleusinian Mysteries*.

demons Despite their popular association with evil in the Judeo-Christian West, 'demon' actually derives from the Sanskrit root *div*, which means 'to shine', through the Greek *daimon* which means 'divine power'. Thus, in ancient Greece, a demon was a divinity or supernatural being rather than a personification of evil or an evil spirit. It was in medieval Europe, with the development of the new science of demonology, that demons became inextricably linked with evil and were classified into elaborate systems and hierarchies of hell and ascribed various forms, attributes, characters, and duties. Sometimes, such demonologies included not only those demons cast out of heaven alongside Lucifer, but also the pagan deities branded devils by the Christian church – leading to the common Pagan claim that the new (Christian) God made devils of the old gods. Demonology is still a part of occult lore, and can be found in such systems as the kabbalah; however, modern magicians regard them as projections of human qualities which can be used to further self knowledge, rather than as embodiments of evil.

deosil Denotes the clockwise direction, the direction in which the sun travels in the northern hemisphere. A dance done deosil thus raises energy. Its converse is widdershins, which goes against the sun, and therefore deosil has often been regarded as the direction of 'good' or 'right hand path' magic, whilst widdershins has been dubbed the direction for 'black' or 'left hand path' magic. In fact, since magic is deemed to be neither good nor bad in Paganism, the direction of movement will depend on the type of magic being worked. Thus, a slow dance to shrink a tumour may be thought more effective if it takes the widdershins direction.

Devil The supreme manifestation of evil in Christianity. In Paganism, there is no supreme manifestation of evil, and Pagans tend to argue that it is necessary to be a Christian in order to believe in the Devil. The Devil thus has nothing to do with Paganism, although he has obviously been associated with witchcraft through demonologies and the Great Witch Hunt of early modern Europe, remnants of which have stuck in the popular imagination and its concepts of witchcraft and Paganism. Pan, god of wild nature, has sometimes been interpreted as a deliberately chosen symbol of opposition to Christianity among occultists, due to Christian associations of Pan's characteristics (cloven hooves, horns) with their image of the Devil. Certainly, this is true of Aleister Crowley, whose Hymn to Pan provoked storms of outrage when it was read out at his funeral in 1947.

Diana   The Roman moon goddess, guardian of virginity, forest huntress, and protector of animals. 'Diana' was named as the witches' goddess by the American folklorist Charles Godfrey Leland in *Aradia, or the Gospel of the Witches* (1899) in which Aradia, Diana's daughter by her twin brother Lucifer, is sent to earth to teach her mothers' magic to the witches of Tuscany.

Dianic Witchcraft   Form of witchcraft which emerged in the USA from the feminist consciousness movement, sometimes called feminist witch-craft. It began when Z. Budapest met with five friends to celebrate the Winter Solstice in Southern California in 1971. Budapest embraced the image of the witch as a symbol of female empowerment, and building on the myth of ancient matriarchy and Gardnerian Wicca she developed a feminist version of Wicca, called Dianic Wicca after Leland's Goddess of the Witches in *Aradia* (1899), Diana the virgin huntress, who lived independently of men. Another Dianic tradition was formed in Dallas, Texas by Morgan McFarland and Mark Roberts in the late 1960s, developing independently of Budapest, though it only later came to be called after Diana. The Dianic Tradition had also been influenced by Starhawk, a non-Dianic witch whose particular commitment to envir-onmentalism and peace protests nevertheless struck a chord.

An increasing number of feminists joined Dianic covens, and by the 1980s feminist witchcraft was the fastest growing segment of the craft in North America. Dianic covens stress the worship of the Goddess, sometimes exclusively, and as such are largely feminist and/or matriarchal in orientation. The emphasis is on rediscovering and reclaiming female power and divinity and consciousness raising. Some Dianic witches call witchcraft Wimmin's Religion, regarding it as a faith in which men should play no part, and others go so far as to say that all women are witches simply because they are female. Budapest defines the Dianic tradition as 'a woman-centred, female-only worship of women's mysteries ... opposed to teaching our magic and our craft to men until the equality of the sexes is reality' (*The Holy Book of Women's Mysteries*). However, there are also covens which do not exclude men, including the MacFarland version of Dianic Wicca and, though the chief emphasis of their worship is upon the Goddess, the Hornèd God also has his role to play. The Dianic Tradition has spread to Europe, but covens are presently far less numerous and tend

49

not to be as militant as their American counterparts, allowing men an equal role in worship, and worshipping both the Goddess and the Hornèd God as her consort.

Dionysus   Greek god of wine and intoxication, ritual madness, and ecstatic liberation; one of the twelve Olympians. The cult of Dionysus was tied to wine-making and involved plays and phallic processions. Beginning in the rural areas, it was later incorporated into city life in Athens, which alone had seven festivals dedicated to him, and the Orphic mysteries then added a new mysticism to the worship of Dionysus, who became the god who is destroyed, who disappears, who relinquishes life and then is born again. Sacred to Dionysus was the ivy-twined, pine-cone tipped staff known as the thyrsus, an obvious phallic symbol which was thought to have magical properties which could be used to obscure the identity of the carrier.

Discworld   A world invented by Terry Pratchett which consists of a disk resting on the backs of four elephants which in turn stand on the back of a giant turtle, called A-Tuin, who floats lazily through space. The discworld is home to numerous characters who have become delightful to Pagans, in particular the witches – Granny Weatherwax, Nanny Ogg, and Magrat Garlick – and the wizards of the Unseen University.

divination   The art of foretelling the future, finding lost property, or identifying guilty persons through such means as astrology, dowsing, dreams, I Ching, Tarot, communication with spirits, oracles, visions, and the reading of auguries.

divine   In Paganism, the Divine is perceived as both immanent and transcendent, interspersed throughout nature through the web of interconnections, but also the unifying whole. All things are therefore dependent on this universal life force. But the life force is also seen as manifesting in many different Gods and Goddesses with whom humans can relate. Such a concept of the divine reflects a broader 'unity in diversity' theme which runs through Paganism, and it would therefore be wrong to say that all Pagans are polytheists, duotheists, pantheists or panentheists. Superficially, for example, Wicca usually appears duotheistic, focusing on the triple Goddess of the Moon (Maiden, Mother and Crone) and the Hornèd God of the woods, the hunt, and Lord of Death. However, in the practical work of ritual the Wiccan worldview is polytheistic – a variety of Gods and Goddesses are used from many different pantheons, the most common being Celtic, Norse, Egyptian, and Greek. Among

Pagans, the same holds true, with some directing their worship toward a single aspect of deity, others focusing on a Goddess and God, and others devoting themselves to an entire pantheon, either from a particular culture or from many cultures. For some, the Gods are archetypes which humans can relate to by virtue of the divine part of ourselves. For others, the Gods are external forces operating in the universe who can manifest through humans. Many Pagans view the Divine as both within humans and external.

dowsing   A method of divining water, using a rod of forked hazel or other wood, metal, or a pendulum. Dowsers are sometimes known as 'water witches'.

Dragon Environmental Network   A Pagan organisation founded as the Dragon Environmental Group in London on July 18th 1990 by Adrian Harris. Its first campaign was to help save Oxleas wood, which still thrives today. The name derives from 'the Dragon' as an ancient name for the energies of the earth: ley lines are sometimes called dragon lines, and the dragon is perceived as representing the dark, hidden power of the earth. Dragon is a Pagan eco-magical group which incorporates magical practice and spirituality into environmental concerns and protests, using rituals geared towards environmental, social and spiritual change, as well as necessary fundraising, conservation, recycling, and educational talks and events to raise awareness. It is committed to non-violent direct action, and open to people of any religion or spiritual path who share a belief in the earth as sacred. The Dragon practice of eco-magic is encouraged as an holistic method of treating the causes of ecological damage in society rather than just the symptoms to be seen in the environment.

Drawing Down the Moon/Sun   Part of a Wiccan ritual in which the priestess and priest receive the goddess and god into them through invocation.

drugs   In theory, drugs are regarded as one of the eight paths of magic in Wicca, but in practice nothing more than wine, beer, or cider tends to be imbibed before or during ritual. Drugs other than alcohol are generally frowned upon before ritual, for ritual is regarded as an effective means of altering one's state of consciousness in its own right, without the need for drugs.

Druids, Druidry   The origins of Druidry are lost in the remote past, though much of modern Druidry draws its inspiration from Celtic traditions. Early evidence of Druidry has been gleaned from the works of writers such as Pliny the Elder and Julius Caesar. The Roman invasions of Gaul and Britain and the introduction of Christianity led to the decline of Druidry in England, but Bardic Colleges in Ireland and Scotland continued until the Sixteenth and Seventeenth Centuries respectively. By this time, antiquarian writers such as John Aubrey (1629–1697), John Toland (1670–1722) and William Stukeley (1687–1765) had revived Druidry in England. This was continued by a Welsh visionary, poet and charlatan, Edward Williams (1747–1822), better known as Iolo Morganwg, whose writings were published as *The Iolo Manuscripts* (1848) and *Barddas* (1862). He concocted rituals for his Gorsedd of the Bards of Britain in 1792 which are still performed today as part of the Welsh Royal National Eisteddfod. The Nineteenth Century revival of interest in Celtic studies provided new impetus to the Druid movement.

In the twentieth century, further revision was undertaken through the writings of Lewis Spence, Ross Nichols and others, with present day writers such as John and Caitlín Matthews and Philip Carr-Gomm continuing the development of the tradition. In 1988, the Council of British Druid Orders was formed and has developed into a body representing around fourteen Druid Orders.

Pagan Druidry tends to be based on the religious traditions of the Celts of Britain and Europe, and on Arthurian legend, but not all Druid groups are Pagan. For the nineteenth and much of the twentieth centuries, Druidry overlapped with Christianity and many Druid orders operated as social or charitable, rather than religious, bodies. It was not until the 1980s that specifically pagan Druidry was developed, with the foundation of orders such as the British Druid Order, which has a shamanic and Wiccan influence. Some are Goddess based, some distinctly Pagan, others distinctly not. Some do not regard Druidry as a religion at all, but as a philosophy or science. Most, however, seek to preserve the ecological balance of the Earth and see humankind as an integral part of nature rather than above or in control of nature.

There is great variety within contemporary Druidry, including Pagan Druids, Christian Druids, Zen Druids and even Hassidic Druids, all with differing levels of commitment, formality and seriousness. Some take a very light-hearted approach, such as the Berengaria Order of Druids which draws its inspiration from sci-fi such as *Star Trek* and *Babylon 5*.

dryads   Tree spirits.

E

earth   Densest of the four classical elements of nature, earth is associated with the colours black and brown, with winter and night, the northerly direction, sensation and practicality, fertility, patience, stagnation, and the zodiacal signs of Taurus, Virgo and Capricorn. Along with water, it is considered to be a feminine element.

east   Direction associated with the element of air, with morning, spring, and colours such as blue and yellow. Its elemental king is Eurus, the Greek name for the east wind.

ecology   Paganism has always had an ecological outlook and philosophy, providing a spiritual context for ecology through its focus on reverence for Nature, the Earth as Goddess and Mother, and celebrations of natural phenomenon such as lunar phases and the changing cycle of the seasons. However, in the last decade or so, Paganism has become much more active in this area, with many Pagan groups becoming involved in animal rights, tree planting, collecting money for buying woods, and actively protesting against road building and other programmes which threaten the environment.

eco-magic   Magical and spiritual action for the environment. See also *Dragon Environmental Network*.

Eddas   Two Icelandic books from the thirteenth century. The *Elder*, or *Poetic Edda* is a collection of old Norse poems on mythical or traditional subjects. The *Younger* or *Prose Edda*, written by the Icelandic historian Snorri Sturluson who felt it was necessary to preserve his people's traditions, contains Icelandic poetry with prosodic and grammatical treatises, quotations and prose paraphrases of old poems. The Eddas constitute the main source of knowledge of Scandinavian mythology.

Egypt/Egyptian Mysteries   The Egyptian Mysteries make use of ancient Egyptian polytheism, popular gods and goddesses today including Anubis, Osiris, Isis, Bast, Hathor, Sekhmet, and Ma'at. The Egyptian Mystery colleges of today draw inspiration from archaeological findings pertaining to religion as practised by the ancient Egyptians, using their own intuition to fill in the gaps. No lineage is claimed back to this ancient civilisation; rather the practitioners see themselves as tuning into an everlasting current of Egyptian wisdom and reviving religious practices in a contemporary context.

In the 1890s, occultists such as Moina and MacGregor Mathers of the Hermetic Order of the Golden Dawn performed rituals to the Egyptian Goddess Isis in Paris and London, and as Egyptology became more established and discoveries in Egypt increased, fascination with this ancient civilisation and its deities likewise grew among members of occult fraternities such as the Golden Dawn and Dion Fortune's Fraternity of the Inner Light. Fortune's books *The Sea Priestess* (1938) and *Moon Magic* (1956) popularised Isis, and are extremely popular among Pagans to this day. Fascination with ancient Egypt has continued up to the present, with the foundation of the Fellowship of Isis (1976) inspired by, though not limited to, the Egyptian Goddess Isis, the appearance of mystery colleges (some of which are affiliated to the Fellowship of Isis as Lyceums or training colleges), and many Wiccan, Magical and other Pagan groups using the religion of Ancient Egypt in their rituals. It is thought by some that the many thousands of years when the Egyptian goddesses and gods were worshipped have enabled them to maintain a very strong grip on the human imagination, often appearing spontaneously in vision and dream, such that many people throughout the world now worship the Egyptian deities either alone or as part of a group.

Egyptian Book of the Dead   More accurately known as the *Book of Going Forth by Day*, the Book of the Dead is a collection of religious and magical texts from ancient Egypt aimed at helping the soul survive the journey through hell (Amenti).

Ehrenreich, Barbara   Co-author, along with Deirdre English, of *Witches, Midwives and Nurses: A History of Women Healers* (1972), a booklet influential to feminist witchcraft, which claimed that the women persecuted as witches during the Great Witch Hunt were in fact the traditional healers and midwives of their day; their destruction was therefore a blow to female power and natural medicine, and established a male-dominated and flawed modern science.

eight fold path   In Wicca, there are thought to be eight paths of realisation: meditation/concentration; trance; rites, chants and spells; incense, drugs and wine; dance; scourging; blood control; and the Great Rite.

elementals   Spirits of the four mundane elements, who are often mischievous. Gnomes are the earth elementals, undines the water elementals, salamanders the fire elementals, and sylphs the air elementals.

Elemental Lords   As part of the ritual framework of Wicca and many magical groups, the 'Lords of the Watchtowers' are invoked at each direction. The 'Lords' are the 'Kings of the Elements', the 'Elemental Lords', or the 'Mighty Ones', and they are invoked to protect and guard the circle. In ritual, the Watchtowers are invoked by facing the appropriate direction, drawing the elemental pentagram in the air with the athame, visualising the image of the Lord of the Watchtower, and summoning the entity to the circle. The elemental lords are named after the Greek winds: Boreas is guardian of the North, Eurus guards the East, Notus the South, and Zephyrus the West.

elements   From Greek philosophy, the name given to earth, water, fire and air (the mundane elements) and aether. In Paganism, particularly in Wicca and Druidry, the balancing of the elements within a person is deemed especially important, being one of the foundation stones of magic and the exhortation 'Know Thyself'.

Eleusinian Mysteries   A mystery cult which thrived in ancient Greece. There is considerable speculation regarding the nature of the Eleusinian Mysteries, which were a closely guarded secret, punishable by death by the Athenian court if anyone probed them. The Mysteries were said to have originated somewhere around 1800 BCE and provided the Greeks with a mystical system equivalent to anything the Egyptians had to offer at the time. When the mysteries were at their height, three grades were involved: the Small Mysteries, the Great Mysteries, and Epoptism. Every respectable citizen of Athens who was not ritually impure and could afford the initiation fee endeavoured to become initiated at the higher or more secret levels, and the Eleusis temple was built to hold ten thousand people. The lesser mysteries were celebrated towards the end of winter, in the town of Agra, a suburb of Athens and anyone, including foreigners, was allowed to attend these. The Greater Mysteries were held in September/October, between the time of harvesting and sowing the new seeds; they were celebrated in Eleusis itself, involving processions and sacrifices of pigs to Demeter, and the enactment of the Demeter/ Persephone legend, but there is much disagreement among scholars and historians regarding what actually took place. Epoptism was considered the highest and most secret initiation to be undergone.

energy   Magical energy is believed to be released from the body. To many witches, being naked, or 'skyclad', allows power to flow from the body unimpeded, and when robes are worn, natural fabrics such as cotton, silk or wool are preferred, as natural fibres are thought to allow magical energy to pass through them. The energy built up in ritual through dancing and chanting is used to draw down divine energy into a priest and priestess who are being invoked, and this energy is in turn channelled into the cakes and wine to bless the sacred meal. Any residual energy is used in spells, for which more dancing and chanting will build up the required level of energy again.

English, Deirdre   See *Ehrenreich, Barbara*.

Enochian Magic   A form of angelic magic discovered and practised by Dr John Dee and Edward Kelly in sixteenth century Elizabethan England.

Eostre   Anglo-Saxon fertility goddess of spring, from whose name Easter is derived. Pagans in North America tend to call the Spring Equinox festival Eostre.

Epona   British and Celtic fertility goddess, associated with the horse and thus adopted by Roman cavalry units. Impressions of her exist in bas reliefs and statues from Gaul, the Danube, the Rhineland, as well as British and Roman. In Rome, she was often called Epona Augusta or Regina.

equinoxes   The two points of the year when the sun crosses the celestial equator, when day and night are of equal length. The vernal equinox occurs c. 21st March in the northern hemisphere (September in the southern hemisphere) and the autumnal equinox c. 21st September (March in the southern hemisphere). They are celebrated by Pagans as two of the festivals of the Wheel of the Year. See also *Autumn Equinox, Spring Equinox*.

esbat   A term introduced by Margaret Murray to denote gatherings of witches for the purpose of business rather than religion. The meaning of the term is not known. It was picked up by Murray from de Lancre, and she then derived it from the French *s'esbattre*, which she translated as 'to frolic'. In modern Wicca, 'esbat' is used as a term for 'moon rituals' which are held between Sabbats (usually every two to three weeks) and where training and instruction are given. Esbats are traditionally held on or near the time of the full moon, after the exhortation in Leland's *Aradia* and Valiente's revision of it as *The Charge of the Goddess* to meet in her holy place 'and better it be when the moon is full'. For some feminist witchcraft groups, the promise of God that women should have the Rosh Chodesh (full moon) as their own lends poignancy to this time of the month.

esotericism A term used to describe teachings which are secret in that they are not revealed to those unfit to receive them, i.e. the uninitiated. More accurately, esotericism refers to the inner or spiritual meaning underlying literal surface meanings. These can be comprehended by the intuition, for they cannot be revealed or explained – rather, they must be grasped through the inner development of each person. See also *Western Esoteric Tradition*.

ethics Perhaps the only rule which approaches universal status is the Wiccan Rede – 'An it harm none, do what ye will' – which has been adopted almost verbatim by the Pagan population in general as the Pagan Ethic. The Rede is purposefully vague, allowing for individual interpretation. Paganism thus has ethics which are neither codified nor enforced. Rather, there is a strong element of individual responsibility, and ethics are not, therefore, something to be carved in stone, as a list of commandments, but are fluid and situational – an absolute or universal ethical code to which all Pagans must adhere would take away the individual responsibility. The Pagan Federation, which has adopted the Rede as a common Pagan ethic over the past thirty years, explains it as a positive morality, expressing the belief in individual responsibility for discovering one's own true nature and developing it fully, in harmony with the outer world and community. The Law of Threefold Return – that what one does to others, whether for good or ill, will come back on one threefold – is another almost universally accepted creed, but again it remains open to widely differing interpretation. To some, it is assimilable with the eastern concept of karma, to others it is the Christian concept of doing unto others as you would have them do unto you. Activities are not governed by overriding rules and regulations. Behavioural rules are generally subtle and seldom need to be made explicit.

evocation The process of conjuring a spirit to physical manifestation.

F

Faery Wicca (Variously spelt, Faerie, Feri) Form of witchcraft developed by Americans Victor and Cora Anderson and Gwyddion Pendderwen in the 1970s as an oral tradition based on the ancient myth of a race of people skilled in magic, healing and crafts, who arrived in Ireland bringing with them a Great Mother Goddess called Dana; they became known as the Tuatha De Danaan, the Tribe of Dana, who eventually retreated into the Otherworld, the World of Faery. Much of the mythology of Ireland is based on stories about the Tribe of Dana, and the Faery Tradition is based on these tales, as well as incorporating Hawaiian Kahuna and 'shamanic' practices. It is polytheistic and does not emphasise male/female polarities as much as other traditions. Nature is honoured and the deities (whose names are secret) personifying the forces of nature, life, fertility, death and rebirth are worshipped. Emphasis is placed upon pragmatic magic, self development and theurgy. It is an initiatory tradition, and thus some material is kept secret though much is taught openly and many of the fundamentals of the tradition have become widespread through the writings of Starhawk, who is an initiate of Faery Wicca. In Britain and Europe, many covens base their rituals on Irish or other Celtic religion and mythology as their natural heritage. They are not necessarily practitioners of the Faery Tradition.

familiars   Agents of witches thought to be given to them by the devil at initiation. Witches were often 'discovered' through searching the body for abnormal warts which were regarded as the devils teats from which familiars suckled. Familiar spirits were often believed to attend a witch in the shape of a cat, dog, toad, imp, raven or other such creature, the black cat being perhaps the most famous example.

Farr, Florence   (1860–1917) Initiate of the Hermetic Order of the Golden Dawn in 1890, who took the magical name *Sapientia Sapienti Dono Data* ('Wisdom is a gift given to the wise'). She was a mystic, author, and actress who sought spiritual as well as physical independence at a time when it was difficult for women to do so. She wrote a novel, *The Dancing Faun* (1894) and two plays, *The Beloved of Hathor* and *The Shrine of the Golden Hawk* (1901). Interested in ancient Egypt and in astral travel, Florence studied at the British Museum, produced flying rolls, and set up the London Adepti, a study group of twelve Golden Dawn members, to study astral magic. In 1894, she was made Praemonstratix (female head) of the Isis Urania Temple of the Golden Dawn, and was deeply offended by the initiation of Aleister Crowley by Mathers in 1899 against her wishes. In 1910 she emigrated to Ceylon and founded a college for girls; she never returned to England, and died of breast cancer aged 57. After receiving a message from her during a seance, Caroline Wise of Atlantis Bookshop arranged for the performance her plays in aid of Breast Cancer Research.

Farrar, Janet and Stewart (Stewart 1916–2000) Prolific Wiccan authors whose many books include *What Witches Do: A Modern Coven Revealed* (1971), *Eight Sabbats for Witches* (1981), *The Witches' Way* (1984), *The Witches Goddess'* (1987), *The Witches' God* (1989), *Spells and How They Work* (1990) and with Gavin Bone *The Pagan Path* (1995) and *The Healing Craft* (1999). *The Witches' Way* contains the bulk of the contemporary Gardnerian rituals, and was published with the active help of Doreen Valiente, who wrote most of them and had herself made a large amount of material available in her 1978 book *Witchcraft for Tomorrow*. It thus made the core ritual format and texts of Gardnerian Wicca available to all. Stewart met Alex and Maxine Sanders whilst working as a journalist in 1969, and was initiated by Maxine in 1970. He and Janet ran their own coven in London, married in 1974, and subsequently moved to Eire in 1976. Stewart also wrote occult novels, perhaps the most well-known being *Omega*.

fasting A well-known method of making the transition to an altered state of consciousness. Some Wiccans fast for a certain amount of time before a ritual. The length of time spent fasting differs depending on the rite: for initiations and sabbats, people tended not to eat for the whole day beforehand, whereas for esbats people often eat lunch and then nothing until the feasting during the ritual.

feasting Eating and drinking after rituals begins the process of returning to everyday reality, and is considered to be essential for 'grounding', coming back into relatively normal space and time, gradually preparing for leaving the ritual space.

Fellowship of Isis Organisation founded at the Spring Equinox of 1976 by the late Lawrence Durdin-Robertson along with his wife Pamela and his sister Olivia, at Huntingdon Castle, Clonegal, Eire, still the Foundation Centre of the fellowship. It concentrates on both female and male principles of divinity and is thus not exclusively orientated to women. With over thirteen thousand members spread over eighty countries, it is the largest Goddess-centred organisation in the world. Both men and women are initiated as priests and priestesses. The Fellowship of Isis stresses its multi-faith and multi-cultural vision, and counts Christians, Hindus, Witches, Pagans, and atheists among its members. All members are considered equal, and there are no vows, hierarchies, dogma, or duty to remain within the Fellowship. Neither is anyone required to abandon their religious beliefs. From the Foundation Centre, the Fellowship has a network of affiliated Iseums, many of which are dedicated to a specific goddess and/or god, and Lyceums of the College of Isis which carry out the liturgy and training of potential priests and priestesses. Correspondence courses are also available, and thirty three Magi degrees reflect the growth of members.

Feraferia US neo-pagan religious movement founded by Frederick Adams, inspired by the work of Robert Graves, William Morris, H. Thoreau, Carl Jung and H. B. Stevens' *The Recovery of Culture*. This latter theorises that the primordial period of the development of the human race was that of the mythical paradise. Following from this, Feraferia ('wilderness festival') celebrates Wilderness Mysteries through a melding of art, ecology, mythology and liturgy.

fertility Initially Gardner's Wicca was described as a fertility cult, concerned with the fertility of the land but also with the fertility of creation within the human, whether that be the birth of children or of an idea, a book, a work of art, poetry etc.

Ficino, Marsilio (1433–1499) Italian philosopher and theologian, famous for his translations of Plato and for his advocacy and interpretation of Platonist thought. In the late fifteenth century, Ficino undertook the translation into Latin of the Greek *Hermetica*, which was brought to Cosimo de Medici in Florence.

Finnish Paganism From the Twelfth Century, Finland was a province of Sweden, Christianised late, and annexed by Russia at the beginning of the nineteenth century. There was no written scripture among the Finno-Ugrian peoples, traditions being transmitted orally until they were written down in poetic form in the *Kalevala* ('Abode of Kalevala', a giant ancestor of humankind) and *Kanteletar* in the early nineteenth century. Elias Lohnrot, who compiled the *Kalevala,* aimed to revive the Finnish sense of national identity; it proved a great stimulus to Finnish nationalism and the revival of the Finnish language and is now the main source of Finnish mythology in the English-speaking world. The impact of the *Kalevala* is apparent from the fact that Kalevala Day (28th February) is now a Finnish national holiday. Finnish cosmology contains three realms – the Upper-world, the Lowerworld or Underworld, and the world of everyday consciousness – which are to be found on a World Tree similar to the Norse Yggdrasil. Some Finnish pagans believe that people's destinies are written in the leaves of this tree, and that when a leaf falls, a person dies.

Modern Pagans in Finland have developed their own seasonal cycle, the major feast of which is Ukon Vakat (Ukko's Day) in honour of the sky and thunder god Ukko; it is held on 4th April and celebrates the end of Spring ploughing. Rites are simple and are often conducted outdoors. In recent years, some Finnish pagans have merged their traditions with those of Wicca, choosing to honour the goddess Mielikki (Spirit of the Forest) and the god Tapio (Old Man or Lord of the Forest) as their principle deities. Due to the geographical proximity of Finland to Siberia and the nomadic way of life which prevailed until relatively recent times, Finnish Paganism has its roots in Shamanism, sharing many similar concepts – such as the honouring of ancestors, spirits of the land, and the elements of earth, air, fire and water – with Siberian and Arctic peoples.

fire One of the four classical elements of nature, associated with the compass direction South and with the colours red, orange, yellow, gold, emotions such as rage and anger, speed, the planet Mars, energy, direction, will, intuition, the wand, and the zodiacal signs of Aries, Leo, and Sagittarius. Along with Air, considered masculine.

first degree The first of three levels of initiation in Wicca, it is the rite by which an individual enters Wicca and becomes a priest/priestess and witch. Its purpose is to open a gateway to spiritual awakening for the individual which they can then choose to walk through 'of their own free will', and to bond the new initiate with other members of the coven. The initiand is required to become vulnerable and enter the magic circle as a child, approaching the circle naked and blindfold as a symbolic representation of their openness and vulnerability as they join the coven. The initiand is also bound with three cords as a symbolic representation of his or her willingness to bond with the coven and, towards the end of the ritual, the initiand's measure is taken and kept by the initiators as a symbolic reminder of the their responsibility towards the initiate, and of the initiate's responsibility to the coven and to Wicca. The measure is usually returned to the initiate after the Third Degree initiation, when the initiate is regarded as fully independent and responsible for him- or herself. Additionally, commitment to the coven, tradition and Wicca as a whole is promoted through intimate communication. This includes the giving of two (traditionally secret, but long-since published) passwords for entering the magic circle at initiation – 'Perfect Love' and 'Perfect Trust'. The concepts of perfect love and perfect trust are mutually accepted by all Wiccans, and are emphasised by the oaths of secrecy and protection taken at initiation. The first degree initiation ritual in Wicca is not only a rite of admission, but is also designed to effect a spiritual transformation in which the status of the initiand changes from that of neophyte to that of Priest or Priestess, from outsider to insider, crossing the protective Wiccan boundaries of secrecy and of the circle. The initiand thus crosses the threshold into the sacred ritual space of the Wiccan circle, and becomes part of the community of both the particular coven into which he or she has been initiated and part of the greater community of Wicca. The initiate thus identifies him- or herself as an initiate of a specific coven and a specific tradition of Wicca.

fith-fath   Also known as a poppet, the fith-fath is a wax or clay doll-like image of a person moulded for use in sympathetic magic. Generally believed to be used for malefic purposes, through sticking pins into the image which would cause a corresponding pain in the body of the person whose image it was, fith faths are usually used for the purposes of distant healing in Wicca. Voodoo, Santeria, Ojibwa and other branches of African magic also employ such images.

five-fold kiss   Wiccan ritual practice in which the body is kissed on each foot, each knee, the genitals or womb, each breast, and finally the lips. It is derived from the Masonic five true points of fellowship.

flagellation   A ritual practice which forms an integral part of some Gardnerian covens where candidates are scourged at each initiation and, sometimes, before each circle or each sabbat. Scourges in Wicca traditionally have eight thongs, and these can range from light threads to leather straps with knots in, and thus have a range of effects. The intent is not, however, to harm but to symbolise purification, (self) discipline, and submission/domination.

flying ointment   Sometimes known as witches' salve, flying ointment was made from fat to which was added certain narcotic herbs such as henbane, deadly nightshade, and thornapple, the properties of which are absorbed into the body through the skin and give the sensation of flying.

flying rolls   Term used in the Hermetic Order of the Golden Dawn to describe papers written as lessons on subjects necessary for the training of members, including administrative details, developing the will, and astral travel. The majority were written by MacGregor and Moina Mathers, Florence Farr, Annie Horniman, Percy Bullock, and Dr Edward Berridge.

folklore   The importance of the study of folklore to the development of Wicca and thence Paganism should not be underestimated. The Folklore Society, established in 1878, has had among its members Gerald Gardner and Margaret Murray, and the research of members into calendar customs, beliefs, charms and magic, local stories, and sacred places have been instrumental in keeping alive and expanding a body of knowledge which Pagans have drawn on and which they themselves add to.

Fordham, Dorothy   See *Clutterbuck, Dorothy.*

Fortune, Dion   (1890–1946) (Born Violet Mary Firth) Prominent occultist and novelist, born in Llandudno into a wealthy Sheffield steel-making family and practised in London as a psychoanalyst prior to the First World War. A member of both the Theosophical Society and of the rival Golden Dawn offshoots, Alpha et Omega and the Stella Matutina, before forming her own Fraternity of the Inner Light in 1924. The Inner Light was intended to bridge the gap between Christian and Pagan doctrines and was based in Glastonbury and then London. Prior to the publication of Golden Dawn rituals by Israel Regardie in 1937–40, the Fraternity of the Inner Light used mainly Golden Dawn rituals and retained relatively strong links with the Stella Matutina. Gradually, however, the Inner Light rituals altered until they bore no resemblance to those of the Golden Dawn. Fortune married a doctor, Thomas Penry Evans in 1927, separated from him in 1937 and divorced in 1945 before her death, in 1946, from myeloid leukaemia. She is buried in Glastonbury.

Fortune's main contribution to the influences on Wicca and Paganism are to be found in her perpetuation of the Western Mystery Tradition and her self-identification as a 'priestess'. Since psychoanalysis was a fad for Fortune's generation, it could also be the case that she began the process of integrating psychology into the current of western esotericism. She does not appear to have considered herself 'Pagan', but many consider her to be a 'proto-Pagan', and her writings, particularly her novels *The Sea Priestess* (1938) and *Moon Magic* (1956), and perhaps her most respected occult work *The Mystical Qabalah* (1935), remain popular with Pagans.

Frazer, Sir James   (1854–1941) Most famous for his volumes of essays published between 1890 and 1915 known as *The Golden Bough*, in which he proposed an evolutionary theory of the development of human thought from the magical and religious to the scientific. At Liverpool University, the first chair in anthropology was created for him, and he is generally regarded as the founder of British social anthropology.

Freemasonry The world's largest secret society, the Fraternal Order of Free and Accepted Masons claims origins in Ancient Egypt, the builders of Solomon's temple in Jerusalem, and the medieval craft guilds of stonemasons who built the great cathedrals of Europe. It was established in Scotland at the end of the sixteenth century, and in its present form in 1717 when the Grand Lodge of London was formed. Freemasonry had a close-knit federal structure, appeared like a counter-Church, and was at first opposed by the Church authorities, a Papal Bull being issued against the movement by Pope Clement XII in 1738. The Masonic movement was attractive because it claimed to be the sole recipient and guardian of an ancient powerful secret handed down from antiquity, an idea which had been popularised earlier by Renaissance scholars.

Freemasonry requires of its members a belief in a Supreme Being, and has three levels of initiation (Entered Apprentice, Fellow Craft, and Master Mason). All initiates take their initiation vows on, or in full view of, the Volume of Sacred Law (i.e. the Bible), membership is composed exclusively of men, discussion of religion and politics is forbidden within the Lodge, and the Three Great Lights of Freemasonry (the Volume of the Sacred Law, the Square and the Compasses) are always exhibited when the Lodges are at work. The Square represents the regulation of actions, symbolising the straight and undeviating line of conduct expected of a Mason. The Compasses symbolise the due bounds of relationship with all mankind and represent the unerring and impartial justice of the Supreme Being, who has defined the limits of good and evil and will reward or punish according to the regard or disregard paid to His commands. Together, they remind Masons to bear in mind, and act in accordance with, the laws of the Divine Creator.

Most of the leading occultists of the Nineteenth Century were members either of Masonic Lodges or quasi-Masonic fraternities, such as Co-Masonry, which allowed women to join them on an equal basis with men. It was a huge influence on the Golden Dawn and upon Gerald Gardner, who incorporated many elements of Freemasonry into Wicca.

Freya Norse goddess, wife and sister of Odin, who flew by means of a falcon-plumed robe. Mother of Baldur. Protectress of marriages, though often unfaithful to Odin herself, she also fought alongside him and commanded the Valkyries.

Full Moon Traditionally the time for esbats, many Pagan meetings are still held at the full moon if possible.

G

Gaia Primordial earth goddess of Greek myth, the first to be born after Chaos came into being. Said to have prophetic powers, she was associated with a number of oracles including that of Delphi, which was said to have been hers originally before she was ousted by the Olympian Apollo, who killed the huge snake Python which Gaia had set there as guardian and took over the oracle. Gaia was worshipped as a fertility goddess throughout Greece, and was associated with Tellus or Terra in Rome.

Gaia hypothesis Theory put forward by the British scientist James Lovelock in 1969. It argues that all living matter on the earth collectively defines and regulates the material conditions necessary for the continuance of life. The earth is thus conceived as a vast self-regulating organism which modifies the biosphere to suit its needs.

galdr Rune chanting. In some Heathen groups, ceremonies often begin with the chanting of an entire set of runes.

Gardner, Gerald (1884–1964) Publicist and perhaps founder of Wicca, born in Great Crosby, Lancashire and spending most of his asthmatic childhood in the care of his nursemaid, Josephine McCombie, going with her to Ceylon in 1900 when she married a tea planter. He taught himself to read and write, and remained in the Far East throughout his working life, moving from Ceylon to Borneo in 1908, and then on to Malay in 1911. In 1927, on a visit to England, he married a nurse called Dorothea Frances Rosedale, usually called Donna, and when Gardner retired in 1936 she insisted that they return to England. In retirement, Gardner lived in Highcliffe and London until moving to Castletown on the Isle of Man in 1954. He visited archaeological sites in the Near East, joined the Folklore Society (being elected to the council in 1946), the Co-Masons, the Rosicrucian Fellowship of Crotona, and the Druid Order. It was the Fellowship of Crotona which allegedly contained a hidden inner group of hereditary witches who initiated him in 1939, and whose rituals he wrote about in fictional form in the novel *High Magic's Aid* (1949) under the pseudonym Scire. The existence of this coven has neither been proved nor disproved.

Gardner claimed that witchcraft had survived the persecutions and persisted in secret throughout history, following the thesis of Margaret Murray. After the repeal of the 1736 Witchcraft Act in 1951, he was able to publish more open accounts of the Craft under his real name in the form of *Witchcraft Today* (1954) followed by *The Meaning of Witchcraft* (1959). *Witchcraft Today* vaulted Gardner into the public spotlight, and he made numerous media appearances promoting Wicca. Both books contained information on the Craft as it existed at that time; in the following years Gardner initiated many new witches and covens sprang up operating according to the outlines provided in Gardner's books. In 1951, Gardner had become associated with the Museum of Witchcraft in Castletown and bought the premises when he moved there in 1954. Donna died in 1960, having never been involved in her husband's interest in Wicca and subsequent revival of it. By the time of his death in 1964, Wicca had become well-established in Britain and had been taken to the United States by Gardnerian initiate Ray Buckland.

Gardnerian Wicca   The original branch of Wicca founded by Gerald Gardner in the 1940s and named after him. Gardnerian Wiccans are those whose initiatory lines descend from Gerald. It remains one of the main forms of Wicca practised today, particularly in Britain. Many Wiccan practices are in fact a synthesis of the Alexandrian and Gardnerian Wicca, and an increasing number of Wiccans are initiated jointly or separately into both traditions, thus tracing their lineage back to both Gardner and Sanders. The differences between the two traditions have been played down, and the similarities and synthesis emphasised to such an extent that some Wiccans claim that there is no difference between them, whilst others retain a 'pure' Gardnerian or Alexandrian practice. Gardnerian Wicca differs from Alexandrian in its emphasis on folk paganism and natural, rather than ceremonial magic.

Garlick, Magrat   The youngest of the witches in Terry Pratchett's Discworld novels, who becomes Queen of Lancre. A desperately earnest New Age witch, and member of the coven Granny Weatherwax swears she hasn't got, none of her ancestors were witches, but Magrat was trained by Goodie Whemper, a research witch. She is an inveterate do-gooder, wears green dresses, a black cloak, and lots of occult jewellery, but refuses to wear a black pointy hat.

garter   Sometimes worn by third degree Wiccan high priestesses, who may add a silver buckle for every coven hived from her. The source for this practice seems to be from Margaret Murray's assertion that the garter was the badge of a witch and that, in order to protect a witch whose garter slipped into view, Edward III established the Order of the Garter. Murray claimed that this revealed him to be either a witch himself or a sympathiser.

geburah   ('strength') 5th sephiroth on the kabbalistic tree of life, situated below Binah on the Pillar of Severity. It brings the vision of power, and is symbolised by the pentagon, sword, spear, scourge and tudor rose.

Gimbutas, Marija   (d.1994) Lithuanian archaeologist who argued for the existence of matrifocal and matrilinear goddess-based societies in ancient times. Her work is of chief importance to groups within feminist witchcraft, goddess spirituality, and the goddess movement, who have used her work to provide a basis for their own image of history and of the yearning for a return to matriarchy in the present. Her own personal leanings towards the myth are expressed in the comment she provided for the back cover of Monica Sjöö and Barbara Mor's *The Great Cosmic Mother* (1987) in which she describes the book as 'a vivid picture of the tragic consequences caused by the savage priests of savage patriarchy'. Gimbutas' archaeological work was also interpreted by other feminist writers such as Mary Daly, Merlin Stone, Charlene Spretnak, and Adrienne Rich in the 1970s and 1980s.

Glastonbury   A town located on the plains of the Somerset levels which is held to be sacred by Pagans, Christians, and various New Age groups. It is variously claimed to be the site of Avalon and the burial of King Arthur, a place visited by Joseph of Arimathea (whose staff grew to become the holy thorn which flowers at the Winter Solstice/Christmas) and/or Jesus, and the heart chakra of Britain/the world. The area is believed to lie at the intersection of powerful ley lines of earth energy, which connect Glastonbury Tor with Stonehenge and Avebury. This intermingling of legends and power centres still draws many pilgrims and visitors to the site, and the town is now settled predominantly by those who feel strongly attracted to the Glastonbury myths. This has led to the entire town becoming a New Age fair almost, with its own 'University of Avalon', now called the Avalon Foundation, offering courses in tarot, shamanism, being a priest/ess, crystal healing, and a variety of forms of counselling and therapy. It is one of the oldest sacred sites in England, and includes the abbey, town, and Glastonbury Tor with its remains of an old church tower. Chalice Well, located at the base of the Tor, is said to have been built by

Druids but its reddish mineral-rich waters tend now to be regarded as the menstrual blood of the Goddess, which are believed to have magical and healing powers. In 1929, it was discovered that natural formations around Glastonbury recreate the twelve signs of the zodiac; the origins of the patterns are unknown, but had been mentioned by Dr John Dee in the sixteenth century. Glastonbury's commercialisation was bemoaned in the 1930s in John Cowper-Powys' *A Glastonbury Romance* (1932). Also famous for the music festival which has been held in fields around Glastonbury almost every year since 1970, and now host to the annual Goddess Gathering each August.

gnome   Earth elemental.

gnosis   Knowledge of spiritual and esoteric mysteries; revealed knowledge of God.

Gnostic Mass   A ritual devised by Aleister Crowley to parallel the Roman Catholic Mass. It was intended to be the central ritual of the O∴T∴O, and contains a list of saints and gnostics. It is now performed by many groups of Pagan affiliation or magical adherence.

Gnosticism   Originally a heretical Christian movement dating from the second century BCE, though partly based on pre-Christian ideas and infused with Greek philosophy and other pagan sources. The power of gnosis to redeem the spiritual in humans was emphasised. They believed in the dualism of a supreme and remote divine being and a demiurge who controlled the world and was antagonistic to all that was spiritual. Christ was seen as an emissary from the supreme divine being, bringing gnosis. Their teachings were known only through the anti-heretical texts of such writers as Iraneus and Tertullian until a collection of Gnostic texts was found near Nag Hammadi, Egypt in 1945–6 and 1948. These latter are known as the Dead Sea Scrolls and have provided a new basis for the interpretation of Gnostic beliefs and influences. Some gnostic ideas remained in later Christian monasticism, or survived among the Mandaeans, adherents of Manichaeism, and Cathars. See also *Jung, C. G.*

Goddess spirituality   Eclectic and loosely structured movement, encouraging creativity and spontaneity and the development of power-from-within rather than power-over others. The Goddess Movement claims to enable women to reclaim their own spirituality, unmediated by male priests, healing the image of the feminine and discovering self-worth and deeper meaning in their own womanhood, and has also helped men to develop a more balanced relationship with the feminine principal. In Goddess spirituality groups, the Goddess is represented as strong and powerful and, likewise, women are honoured as Priestesses, women of power, as active and energising as the Goddess. As well as working within various Pagan traditions, many women have established their own traditions, often strongly connected to feminist movements. Self-identity and strength has been developed from the Women's Movement, leading more and more women to Goddess spirituality and a rediscovery of ancient knowledge of womanhood and the innate powers of the female. Many groups of women meet and perform rites drawing upon Wicca, shamanism, classical paganism, Native American Indian traditions and others to worship the Great Goddess in a context which meets the needs of women in modern life. Some regard themselves as a sisterhood, in which the older women teach the younger women and conduct rites of passage for menarche, childbirth, menopause and other transitions in a woman's life.

goddesses/gods   Female and male deities. There is no omnipotent divine being in Paganism as there is in monotheistic religions. Instead, gods and goddesses are perceived as expressions or symbols of the divine, usually having a specific area of influence in keeping with their original roles in various pantheons but also taking in modern culture, modern needs, and the development of psychology. See also *divine* and various gods and goddesses mentioned by name (*Aradia, Astarte, Inanna, Cernunnos, Herne, Pan* etc.).

Goetia   See *Lemegeton*.

Gorsedd   (Welsh, 'throne') Council of (traditionally) Welsh bards and Druids, particularly applied to meetings held before the Eisteddfod. The first Druidic Gorsedd was held on Primrose Hill in London at the autumn equinox in 1791, and was affiliated to the Welsh Eisteddfod ('session') in 1819. The Eisteddfod – an annual festival of musical and poetic competitions – dates from the twelfth century, and was revived in the nineteenth century. It is still held annually in Wales to promote Welsh language and culture.

Gorsedd Prayer   Prayer attributed to the bard Talhaiarn but probably written by Iolo Morganwyg. It is still popular among contemporary Druids, and is often spoken at the beginning of ritual. Ross Nichols,

Chosen Chief of the Order of Bards, Ovates and Druids from 1964 to 1975, adapted the last line to read:
>Grant, O God/dess, thy Protection
>And in protection, Strength,
>And in strength, Understanding,
>And in understanding, Knowledge,
>And in knowledge, Knowledge of Justice,
>And in knowledge of justice, to Love it
>And in the love of it, the love of all Existences,
>And in love of all existences, the Love of God/dess and all Goodness.

Gothar   Plural of the Germanic word for priest, *gothi* (male) and *gythja* (female) which is used by some Heathens. Others use the Icelandic *Godar, Godi* and *Gyoja*. The Ring of Troth render the terms as 'Godmen' and 'Godwomen'.

Gothar, Court of   Ruling Council of the Odinic Rite, which consists of nine members who meet each month.

grail   The legend of the grail is important to some Pagans as it is to some Christians, although rather than being the cup used by Christ at the Last Supper, or used to catch the blood of Jesus hanging on the cross, the grail is regarded as either a symbol of the Goddess or as one of the magical totems of the British Isles. See also *cauldron, Arthur, Glastonbury*.

Graves, Robert   (1895–1985) English author and poet of Irish descent who wrote the influential 'historical grammar of mythic poetry', *The White Goddess* (1948). His theory of poetry originating in the praise and service of the moon goddess in the classical ancient world, and his use of Celtic poetry attributed to the Welsh bard Taliesin, Celtic calendar alphabets, the *Mabinogion* etc. have made it a classic source book for Wicca, Druidry and other traditions of Paganism. It was certainly an influence on Gardner and his 'revival' of Wicca.

Great Rite   Sometimes called the Sacred Marriage or *hieros gamos*, the Great Rite is a magical act of ritual sex, performed either symbolically (in token) or in actuality (in true), in which the priest and priestess join together as God and Goddess and become one. In Wicca, the Great Rite in true takes place only between couples, and in private, and is a central part of the third degree initiation. As the Greek *hieros gamos*, the Great Rite is reputed to be an ancient rite which constituted the ultimate religious experience in many Pagan religions, including the Eleusinian and Isian Mysteries, and was an important theme in Celtic mythology bound up with the sanctity of sovereignty where kings performed the Sacred Marriage with the Goddess of the land through her priestess or her symbolic animal. The Sacred Marriage is echoed in the union of the soul with the divine in mystical traditions.

Great Witch Hunt   A name used to denote the witchcraft persecutions of early-modern Europe, also called the Witch Craze and the burning times, perhaps the most important epoch with which contemporary witches identify. During a period of some three hundred years, from the beginning of the fifteenth century to the end of the seventeenth century, an exaggerated nine million women were said to have been put to death. An elective affinity with the image of the witch during the time of the persecutions is commonly regarded as part of the reclamation of female power, a psychological link which is used by modern feminist witches as an aid in their struggle for freedom from patriarchal oppression. The past is focused on as a central source of meaning, where the 'burning times' is used as a rallying symbol, and the witch is regarded both as a martyr and as a symbol of repressed female power. Some feminist witches identify themselves as direct inheritors of a corpus of occult knowledge passed on from the witches of the 'Burning Times': the Hungarian-born Zsuzsanna Budapest, in an interview with *Whole Earth Review* (Spring 1992: 42), passionately exclaimed, '[m]y European ancestors and yours risked the Inquisition's stakes and racks to keep alive a body of knowledge about power and healing. My generation of witches is making this wisdom accessible to those who seek a spiritual foundation for political work'.

Apart from the use of the witch figure as an image of female power however, there was another reason for forging affinities with the witches of the burning times. Identification with those persecuted was, to a certain extent, understandable before the repeal of the 1736 Witchcraft Act in 1951. Until 1951, witchcraft was still illegal, and was punishable, albeit not in terms of death by either hanging or burning. However, even after the 1951 repeal which encouraged Gardner to publicise Wicca and, indeed, to the present day, many witches still fear the subtle persecution of being forced out of jobs or losing their children through trumped-up charges if they are publicly known as a witch.

Greater Sabbat   A name sometimes used to denote the cross-quarter day festivals of Candlemas, Beltane, Lammas, and Hallowe'en. These are also known as the Celtic Fire Festivals.

Green Man   Regarded as a blatantly Pagan image, the Green Man can be seen staring down from the corbels and capitals of churches all over Britain and Europe. Usually carved as a man's face sprouting leafy foliage, he is often perceived as a symbol of life in death and death in life, and has been linked to such figures as Robin Hood, Pan, the Oak King and the Holly King. The name was coined by Lady Raglan in 1939, and quickly adopted by other writers and researchers, but no one knows who he is or what these faces – in places of Christian worship – were supposed to achieve. Neither is there any evidence for his link with Jack-in-the-Green or the other characters mentioned above. Nevertheless, according to *The Encyclopedia of Folklore* 'the aura of mystery in the name and its harmony with current ecological concerns have endeared it to many, and 'The Green Man' will probably prove to be an unshakeable element in the popular concept of 'folklore' (2000: 155). And of course, 'The Green Man' has long been a popular name for that most sacred of Pagan places, the pub!

Green, Marian   Well-known and long-standing member of the Pagan revival in the UK, Marian Green has been the editor of *Quest* magazine since 1970 and runs correspondence courses and workshops in Britain, Europe and Canada. She has studied natural magic from childhood. Her books include *A Witch Alone: Thirteen Moons to Master Natural Magic* (1991), *The Path Through the Labyrinth* (1994), and *The Elements of Natural Magic* (1999).

green religion   Paganism is often promoted by its members as 'green religion' because of its emphasis on nature and ecological concerns.

grimoire   Book containing spells and details of rituals used in magic, the *Key of Solomon* and the Grimoire of Pope Honorious III (1216–1227) being perhaps the most famous. Many grimoires circulated in the medieval period as handbooks of magic, drawing on sources from ancient Egypt, Greek, Hebrew and Latin texts. Some material from these grimoires has found its way into the Wiccan Book of Shadows.

grimsrular   Heathen name for shamanistic warrior-priests who are also skilled in rune-lore.

grounding   Return to everyday waking consciousness after ritual, magical working, pathworking, visualisation or meditation, usually aided by eating and drinking.

group mind A term borrowed from Jungian psychology and used in some Wiccan covens to describe the melding of minds of coven members. The barriers between the psyches of the individual coven members are broken down so that a part of each person's consciousness is fused into a group mind. This is thought to aid non-verbal communication within the group, enable the apprehension of group symbols, and increase the effectiveness of magic and ritual work as the group operates as more than the sum of its individual components. The group mind is thus thought to exist on the border of the personal and collective unconscious, and creates strong bonds between group members.

grove Name used for a group of Pagan Druids, taken from the small woods or groups of trees (*nemetons*) in which Druids were traditionally said to gather.

Gundestrap Cauldron See *cauldron*.

H

hag The third aspect of the triple goddess often perceived as dark and destructive, wielder of the sickle at Lammas, but also as wise woman, the transformer who leads the sacrifice through death and into new life. She thus holds the secrets of life and death, and is queen of the underworld. Her names are many and varied, and include Hecate, Cybele, Kali, Cailleach.

Hallowe'en The cross-quarter day festival of 31st October, also called Samhain by Pagans desiring a more Celtic version of Paganism, and this has become almost ubiquitous. However, Hallowe'en was the common name for the festival before the Celticisation of the last decade really began to influence Paganism, and there are many Wiccans who still call the festival Hallowe'en rather than Samhain. Samhain ('Summer's End'/ 'Summer's Rest') is, however, the Irish name for 1st November, or even for the whole month of November, rather than for 31st October which had a separate name, 'oidhche Mongfind', Mongfind's Night. Its Welsh name is Nos Galan Gaeaf, Winter's Eve, this latter reflecting the two season division of the year into Winter and Summer before the concepts of Spring and Autumn arrived with Graeco-Roman culture. However it is called, the festival is a time for honouring death as part of life, for it is the last Autumn festival before winter really sets in. The land grows barren and the Goddess and God rule in the underworld. Perhaps the most well-known of the Sabbats, Hallowe'en is the time when the veil between the worlds is regarded as thin and the spirits of the dead roam free. For some Pagans, this is a time to remember their ancestors or those who have recently died. Since most Pagans believe in reincarnation, there is not generally an expectation that those long dead will return to visit, for they will have reincarnated. But it is a time for remembrance, and for facing one's own mortality – death is honoured as part of life. Belonging to no-time, Hallowe'en is neither past nor future, and it is therefore a traditional time for divination and games such as apple-bobbing, which symbolise fishing for nourishment in the subconscious or the other world, as well as providing mirth after what can often be a heavy and serious ritual. Many Pagans turn their attention inward, consolidating events of the previous year, assessing their own growth and development, and preparing for the Spring, thus reflecting nature in their own lives, allowing activity to go on beneath the surface just as the earth appears barren but in fact much is happening at root level.

Hammarens Ordens Sällskap ('In the Company of the Order of the Hammer') Heathen group centred around the Wirral, though originating among Swedish families as an Archaic Order of Heathen Geomann Cniths ('Yeoman Knights'). It has a particular affinity to the Norse god Thor but is nevertheless polytheistic. Its primary concern is ecological and, considering Paganism to be removed from the land and nature through the use of an altar, the *Hammarens* do not regard themselves as 'Pagan'. Their aim is to re-establish a yeomanry of self-sufficient organic farmers, and the vanir earth gods are thus important because of their connection with the land. This emphasis is reflected in the group's motto, *Lif ok Lifthrasir* ('life and survival'), which they claim is the key to the revitalisation of the British people, the World Tree, and the gods, and in the use of the bear and the ox, representing land and culture, as their symbols. They consider multiculturalism and homosexuality to be the cause of confusion and problems and desire an end to immigration since they believe that a people's identity derives from the land; if the land is left, then people's well-being is damaged. The Order does not believe in Odin, considering the concept of an 'all father' to be a Christian addition.

handfasting   Pagan marriage ceremony, which can contain vows lasting for a year and a day, a lifetime, or for all lives to come. The usual vow is to stay together for as long as love lasts, after which each is permitted to leave the relationship and go their separate ways. A handfasting is sometimes dissolved by a ritual of handparting. The tradition of a year and a day seems to have originated in the 'greenwood marriages' of May Eve.

healing   An important field in Wiccan and Paganism. Healing for the planet and for people and animals is considered part of the Pagan attitude of concern for all life, and healing techniques from the present and from ancient times are utilised, including auric healing, herbs, crystals and stones, chakras, spells, fith faths, shiatsu, reflexology, acupuncture etc.

Heathens/Heathenism   Term which equates with the Latin 'Pagan', coined by the Goths and used throughout the Germanic languages in the Middle Ages to indicate a follower of a non-Christian religion. People and groups who are drawn to Anglo-Saxon, Germanic and Scandinavian traditions and languages prefer to be called Heathen rather than Pagan; some also call themselves by a more specific name, such as Asatrú or Odinist. In some cases, Heathens regard themselves and their traditions as something distinct from Paganism, whilst others are happy to see themselves as something distinct *within* Paganism. Thus, whilst some share the eight-fold Wheel of the Year with Pagans, others regard this as too Celtic in its influences and prefer to celebrate festivals which they feel are more closely linked with their Anglo-Saxon, Germanic and Scandinavian ancestry, such as Winternights. Many Heathens are particularly concerned with ecology and conservation, and regard Paganism as too removed from the land, which is perceived as the crux of a people's identity. This attitude towards the land has led to some Heathens embracing right-wing views regarding race and sexuality, and their relationship with Paganism can therefore be quite fraught. However, it would be wrong to generalise such attitudes across all Heathens, and inaccurate to view the entirety of Heathenism as the right-wing extreme of Paganism. Just as Paganism embraces people of many political orientations, so too does Heathenism as a distinct group within the Pagan revival. See also *Asatrú; Hammarens Ordens Sällskap; Germanic Paganism; Odinic Rite; Odinism; Odinshof; Ring of Troth; Rune Gild UK.*

Hecate   One of the Greek moon goddesses, along with Artemis and Selene, associated with pathways and crossroads travelled by night, magic and witchcraft. Thus, offerings were often left to her at roadside junctions, and she was regarded as a goddess of witches such as Medea and Circe (her High Priestesses) in the myths of ancient Greece. Sometimes accompanied by a black dog or snakes, she is often depicted carrying a torch. In parts of Thessaly she was reputedly worshipped by occultist moon worshippers. Linked to Persephone and Demeter, she plays a role in the seasonal return of Persephone in some versions of the legend. A crone, or hag goddess.

hedgewitchcraft Usually solitary practitioners, who operate with no hierarchy or organisational structure, do not necessarily regard witchcraft as a religion, and therefore may, or may not, honour gods and goddesses. Where witchcraft is seen as religious practice, a ritual of self-dedication to a particular god and/or goddess may be performed rather than an initiation. Hedgewitches perceive Wicca as the organised form of witchcraft, operating almost as an institutionalised religion, and in order to distance themselves from this they identify themselves as witches, hedgewitches, ditch witches or green witches rather than as Wiccan. They have little in common with Wiccan history or the myths of feminist witchcraft, but rather regard themselves as the modern version of the cunning man or wise woman. The heritage of hedgewitches is thus drawn from the lore of the cunning folk, who were believed to be the wise people in particular rural locations to whom people would turn for healing, midwifery, fertility spells, charms and blessings. Magic and spells used in this tradition thus tend to be natural, based on a knowledge of herbalism, the phases of the moon, and the seasonal cycle of the earth.

During the period of the witch persecution, the witch-finders' saying that "Thou canst not be a witch alone" became popularly believed and solitary witchcraft became ever more hidden. This has led to claims in revivalist witchcraft that only a witch can make a witch and the belief that one has to belong to a coven in order to be a real witch. However, in recent years there has been an upsurge in interest in and numbers of solitary witches. Some have been able, in rural areas, to learn their art as an apprentice from an experienced hedgewitch in the traditional way. Others are witches who prefer the old-style natural way of working to the more ritualistic approach adopted in Gardnerian and Alexandrian Wicca and their offshoots, finding a wealth of knowledge in old herbal almanacs such as Culpeppers and in recent publications, as well as in observing and attuning themselves with nature. Yet others may have been initiated into a coven but found that due to distance or the break up of a coven, it is impossible for them to meet regularly and so work alone, perhaps joining together only for certain festivals or to perform a particularly important piece of work. Thus, solitary witches usually work either entirely alone or with their partner as a couple. In 1994, the Association of Solitary

Hedgewitches (ASH) was established as a contact organisation for witches working alone to make contact with each other in order to share experiences and ideas.

heiros gamos   See *Great Rite*.

Hereditary witchcraft   Witches who claim to follow old practices which are believed to pre-date Gerald Gardner's Wicca, and claim an ancestor or lineage of ancestors who were initiated witches. They are normally initiated into the Craft by a family member, with mothers initiating daughters and fathers initiating sons. Hereditary and Traditional covens are generally run by the High Priest rather than the High Priestess, and they tend to work robed rather than skyclad, preferring a black hooded cloak or robe. Their traditions tend to be handed down in family lines, though not necessarily from parent to child – being born into a family of witches was no guarantee of being trained in the secrets of the Craft. In some instances, a witch decides that none of her children are suitable for the Craft, and instead chooses to initiate a grandchild, so the art skips a generation. It was seldom that anything was handed down in written form, but ritual objects were often inherited.

Hermes   Greek messenger of the gods (Mercury in Rome), also associated with Loki in Norse mythology and with Thoth in Egyptian myth.

Hermes Trismegistus   Greek derivation of the Egyptian god Thoth, tutelary deity of writing, learning, magic, philosophy, and mysticism. In Hermetic literature, he is described as a sage. 'Trismegistus' means 'thrice great', and was an epithet of Thoth in Upper Egypt. See also *Corpus Hermeticum; hermeticism.*

hermeticism, hermetic   Intellectual study of magic which began in Renaissance Italy with Ficino after he had translated the Greek manuscript of the *Corpus Hermeticum*, the body of lore attributed to Hermes Trismegistus. Hermeticism eventually spread throughout western Europe, including England, and even though its pre-Christian provenance was disproved by Isaac Casaubon in 1614, remains popular to this day.

Hermetic Order of the Golden Dawn   Magical and occult order founded in London in 1888 on the basis of fragments of rituals from an unknown German occult order discovered by Dr. William Wynn Westcott, a London coroner and Rosicrucian, in 1887. S. L. MacGregor Mathers fleshed out the fragments into full scale rituals, based largely on Freemasonry, and papers were then forged to give the Golden Dawn a history and authenticity, including a paper showing that Westcott had been given a charter to establish an independent lodge in England. It was on such dubious grounds that the Isis Urania Temple of the Hermetic Order of the Golden Dawn was established in London in 1888, with Westcott, Mathers and Dr. W. R. Woodman, Supreme Magus of the Societas Rosicruciana in Anglia, as the three chiefs. An elaborate hierarchy was created consisting of ten grades or degrees, each corresponding to the ten sephiroth of the Tree of Life of the Kabbalah. These grades were divided into three orders, the Outer, the Second and the Third. The secret society quickly caught on, and three hundred and fifteen initiations took place during its heyday (1888–1896).

By 1897, however, schisms were forming. Followers of Mathers left to form the Alpha and Omega Temple, and in 1903, others left to form a group with the name of the Golden Dawn intact but with the emphasis on mysticism rather than magic. In 1905, a further break came with the founding of the Stella Matutina (Order of the Companions of the Rising Light in the Morning), and though in 1917 the Isis Urania Temple was revived as the Merlin Temple of the Stella Matutina, it went into decline in the 1940s after Israel Regardie, a former member, published its secret rituals.

The Golden Dawn, at its height, possessed the greatest known repository of Western magical knowledge, and redefined the British occult world for the Twentieth Century. The Order has been revived in recent years as The Oxford Golden Dawn Occult Society (OGDOS) in Britain and the New Reformed Order of the Golden Dawn in the USA. OGDOS aims to provide accurate information in order to promote wider understanding of the occult. Its main interests include ceremonial magic, witchcraft, kabbala, tantra, shamanism, and the Thelemic magic of Aleister Crowley.

A candidate for admission into the Golden Dawn had to acknowledge his or her belief in the existence of a 'supreme being', but the old pagan gods were very welcome. Indeed, the Golden Dawn formulae for uniting with the divine was essentially pagan, using pre-Christian practices and names of power found in Hebrew, Greek, Coptic, Egyptian, and Chaldean sources. The Golden Dawn was ahead of its time in recognising the importance of the feminine aspect of the divine, and was founded to include both men and women on a basis of perfect equality.

Hermetic Society Occult organisation founded in 1884 by Anna Kingsford, after resigning as president of the London Lodge of the

Theosophical Society because of its emphasis on eastern philosophies. The Hermetic Society was intended to promote western occultism built on Christian foundations in order to attract intellectuals who had been disturbed by the Darwinian controversy. Kingsford's society may have been the catalyst for the establishment of the Hermetic Order of the Golden Dawn.

Herne An aspect of the Hornèd God, also referred to as Herne the Hunter, perceived to be the leader of the phantom Wild Hunt which is particularly associated with Windsor Great Park in Berkshire, where the park's preserved ancient oak forests are believed to be his domain. Celtic or Anglo-Saxon in origin, he is a chthonic god of the underworld. Herne the Hunter's popularity was given a boost by the 1980s TV series *Robin of Sherwood*, in which the stag-headed god of the forest, and Robin's father, featured predominantly as the spirit and guardian of the forest.

hex Spell, almost synonymous with 'curse' but can also designate a beneficial spell.

hexenbanner Name for cunning people in Germany.

High Magic's Aid Historical novel written by Gerald Garner under the pseudonym Scire, published in 1949, which purports to contain descriptions of the continued practice of medieval witchcraft rites in the New Forest coven into which he had been initiated. Wicca was to be based upon these rites.

High Priest In Alexandrian and Gardnerian traditions, a male Wiccan of second degree or above is given the title High Priest. Thus, a High Priest does not necessarily run the coven but is expected to take on duties and responsibilities within the coven (such as training those with less experience) and in the Wiccan community as a whole. The second degree initiation transmits the lineage and power of the tradition, thus making a High Priest entitled to initiate others up to and including second degree.

High Priestess As above. In some traditions of feminist witchcraft, the position of High Priestess is accorded to whoever is running the ritual, and this is rotated through the membership.

hive-off, hiving Term used to describe the process by which Second or Third degree Wiccans leave the coven into which they were initiated to form their own coven.

hod ('glory') 8th sephiroth on the kabbalistic tree of life, forming the left leg of Adam Kadmon, the primal man. It is related to the realm of the mind and science, the rules and logic of the material world.

Holly King   In some Wiccan and Pagan groups, the tides of the year are reflected in a myth of fraternal rivalry between the Holly King and the Oak King, a story which was popularised in Janet and Stewart Farrar's *Eight Sabbats for Witches* (1981). The Oak King is the God of the Waxing Year, and the Holly King is God of the Waning Year, perceived as light and dark twins, who are both each other and eternal rivals for the favour of the Great Mother Goddess, conquering and succeeding each other as the years go by. At the peak of their half-yearly reign, each King is sacrificially mated with the Goddess (at Beltane for the Oak King, and Lammas for the Holly King), dies, and is resurrected to complete his reign. Thus, at Yule or Midwinter the Holly King is slain by the Oak King, who is in turn ousted by the Holly King at Midsummer.

homosexuality   A criticism of Wicca has been its traditional insistence on gender polarity within the circle, which seemed to deny membership to homosexuals and ignore the polarity within individuals. However, it is rare that covens insist on an equal number of male and female members, or that these members be in couples or that they be heterosexual. Gays, lesbians, and bisexuals are therefore welcome within Wicca, and within feminist witchcraft, particularly the Dianic tradition, lesbians and bisexual women have been dominant. Within Paganism as a whole, groups have been established specifically for gays, lesbians and bisexuals, such as Hoblink (founded in 1989) which offers specialist support for those within Pagan traditions and the occult, and Pagan HIV and AIDS Network (PHAN).

Hopkins, Matthew   (d. 1647) Puritan witchhunter active in Essex and the London area during the English Civil War. Hopkins was responsible for so many convictions and executions that he became known as the Witchfinder General. In 1647 he wrote a treatise called *Discoverie of Witches* and employed a team of assistants to help him cover the whole of southern England. He died, possibly of consumption, his fanatical zeal having made him unpopular, and reaction to his excesses led the number of convictions to wane dramatically.

Hornèd God   Male deity of Wicca and consort of the Goddess. The Hornèd God is a varied, composite figure, representing a solar and vegetation god drawn from Cernunnos, Herne, Odin/Woden and aspects of dying and rising gods such as Osiris, Attis, and Dumuzi. He is also seen throughout the year as the Oak King, Green Man, Sun King, Corn King, Holly King, Hunter, Lord of Death and the Underworld, and the Child of Promise. His journey around the Wheel of the Year is regarded by some Wiccans as a reflection of the human journey through life.

Horniman, Annie (1860–1937) Notable occultist and member of the Golden Dawn, daughter of the founder of the Horniman Museum in Forest Hill, London. She persuaded her father to employ S. L. MacGregor Mathers as a curator and facilitated his marriage to Moina Bergson, with whom she had become friendly when both were students at the Slade School of Art. She subsequently funded the Mathers for many years, when they lived in Paris, but eventually became disillusioned with MacGregor Mathers and his continual pecuniary demands, resigning her position in the Isis Urania Temple in 1896 and then being expelled from the Order by Mathers. W.B. Yeats reinstated her when he took over as Chief of the Order in 1902, but she resigned for good in opposition to the secret groups which continued to exist within the Golden Dawn. She was a patron of the arts, founding two world-renowned theatres – the Abbey Theatre in Dublin and the Gaiety Theatre in Manchester – and the modern English repertory movement.

Horseman's Word, Society of Nineteenth-century society based on the Miller's Word, used to train horsemen and regulate competition for jobs amongst those working with horses in Scotland which then spread into England. The 'horse-whisperers' claimed to be able to gain magical control of a horse through the utterance of a certain word, and claimed an ancestry (from Cain) far older than the Freemasonry which both it and the Miller's Word imitated.

Horus Falcon-headed Egyptian deity, the posthumous son of Isis and Osiris, who avenges his father's death. Regarded as the protector of the monarchy, the living pharaoh was associated with Horus, and the dead pharaoh identified with Osiris. Horus was particularly important to Aleister Crowley, who saw himself as the prophet of the new aeon, the age of Horus.

House of the Goddess A goddess-centred group established by Clan Mother Shan Jayran in 1985 in Balham, London. HOG emphasised women's mysteries and held evening classes and rituals, as well as organising and hosting an annual Hallowe'en festival, one of few large open Pagan gatherings in the 1980s. Shan gives workshops, counselling, and acts as a celebrant at handfastings, funerals etc., offering a feminist and psychotherapeutic approach to Paganism drawn from her identification as a Dianic and shamanic witch.

Howard, Michael   Prominent member of the occult and Pagan communities since the 1960s, and editor of the magazine *The Cauldron* since it was founded in 1976.

Hutton, Ronald   Professor of History at the University of Bristol, and author of a number of leading academic works on Paganism including *The Pagan Religions of the Ancient British Isles* (1991), *Stations of the Sun* (1996), *Triumph of the Moon* (1999), and *Druids, Witches and King Arthur: Studies in the Human Imagination* (forthcoming). A staunch supporter of the academic study of Paganism, he has shared his research at a multitude of Pagan and academic conferences and regularly appears on television, radio broadcasts, and in newspaper articles.

I

Imbolc   One of the four Greater Sabbats of the Wheel of the Year, Imbolc celebrates the first stirrings of spring as the life-force gathers its strength for the coming year. It is regarded as a 'fire festival', the name given to the cross-quarter days between the solstices and equinoxes, but the emphasis is on light rather than heat – the strengthening spark of light that was born at Yule. It is often celebrated as a festival of inspiration, dedicated to Bride, goddess of healing, smithcraft and poetry. The Goddess returns, no longer the hag of the underworld, but the maiden bringing the promise of spring in her wake, and the God who was born at Midwinter is separated from the Mother in order to grow. It is considered to be a time to return from hibernation and begin the new year in earnest, and in Wicca is also a traditional time for initiation, expressing hopes for personal change as inner intentions emerge into outer manifestation. See also *Candlemas*.

Inanna   ('Lady of Heaven') Goddess originating in Uruk, Sumerian Queen of Heaven and mother goddess with whom Ishtar was assimilated. Daughter of Enki, the god of wisdom, Inanna was associated with the seasonally dying vegetation god Dumuzi (Tammuz) whom she sought in the underworld. She ruled over the earth, grain, date palms, wine, weaving, love, oracles, and battles. She was also a goddess of sovereignty, and her sacred marriage with the god, enacted by king and priestess and known as the Enitum, was an annual Sumerian ritual of great importance.

incantation Formula of words repeated in a chant, usually as part of the performance of ritual, to produce a magical effect. It includes spoken spells or charms, and is linked to such other words as chant and enchant. Its purpose is not only to make a link with spirits or deities but to summon or placate them, and is based on belief in the creative power of sound. Incantations enable the exaltation of consciousness through rhythm and repetition in order that the practitioner might address the gods, experience revelations of a mystical nature, or release magical energies in a spell or charm. An incantation can take the form of a prolonged piece of poetry or it can be based on the repetition of names, such as the Kabbalistic names of God (e.g. Adonai, Elohim). Alternatively, incantations consisting wholly of nonsense, foreign, ancient or forgotten languages to achieve a mental state in which consciousness is altered or attuned have been argued to be efficacious.

incense Gums, resins, herbs and spices are mixed into incenses for various rituals according to their magical properties, and burned on charcoal blocks. The scent released can help with changing states of consciousness in rituals, whilst the smoke symbolises the connection between humans and the gods.

individuation Jungian concept utilised by some Wiccans. In order to individuate, one must become a whole person which necessitates an awareness of the shadow, the anima/animus, the ego, the unconscious etc. It is believed that being invoked as different gods and goddesses can help with the process of individuation.

initiation Rite of entry into a Wiccan coven, which in Britain have three levels of initiation (1st, 2nd and 3rd degree). Non-initiates are often not permitted within a Wiccan circle, unless they have been through a neophyte initiation when they may be allowed to observe ritual, and they are never allowed to be present at an initiation before their own. Entry into Wicca, by means of initiation, cannot be offered but must be asked for 'of one's own free will and accord'; the ultimacy of the decision to become a member of the community of a particular coven sits squarely with the individual's assent. Some other Pagan groups, including magical groups and some Druid orders, also practice rites of initiation.

inner planes   See *astral plane*.

intuition   Immediate insight or apprehension which bypasses reasoning. Linked to the element of fire, and one of the four Jungian functions.

invocation   Technique by which the spiritual force of the divine is believed to be drawn into the body of a priestess and priest, a process also known as 'Drawing down the Moon/Sun'. The priest or priestess who is to be invoked stands before the altar and empties their mind, becoming still, becoming an empty vessel which the divine can enter. The invoker kneels before the priest/ess and uses the words of an invocation to imagine a visual image of the deity, visualising the image forming behind the body of the priest/ess and then merging into his or her aura. The energy of the divine is held within the body of the priest/ess who, for the duration of this time, is considered to *be* the Goddess or God. In the practice of invocation, Wiccans perceive themselves to be merging with the divine, becoming attuned to their own divine self and so manifesting part of their own nature by temporarily incarnating the divine.

Ishtar   Babylonian and Assyrian goddess, personification of the planet Venus, who has multiple attributes – earth, fertility, love, marriage, as well as battles and storms, the moon and divination. She corresponds to Astarte.

Isis/Aset   Egyptian goddess who earned the epithet 'Goddess of Ten Thousand Names' because of her multifaceted image and associations. She was worshipped for over three thousand years, and was not limited to Egypt. After the death of Alexander the Great, his successor, Ptolemy I revealed the importance of Egyptian religion to Greece by incorporating the Egyptian cults of Isis and Osiris (now called Serapis) into Greek religion in the fourth century BCE. The cult spread rapidly throughout the Mediterranean and from there throughout the Roman Empire, reaching as far from Egypt as Britain, with centres in London and York. As late as the sixth century she continued to be worshipped at the temple of Philae in Upper Egypt. Isis and Osiris ruled Egypt and taught the Egyptian people all the skills needed for civilisation. But Isis is also associated closely with Thoth, who taught her magic (she tricked the sun god Ra into revealing to her his secret name, and thus gained unsurpassed power). She was a compassionate, motherly goddess who understood suffering because she herself had suffered the murder of her husband and the lengthy search for the pieces of his body. Eventually, Isis absorbed the attributes of many goddesses, and was specifically assimilated with Hathor, goddess of fertility, motherhood, love and joy. Her name, meaning 'throne', made her goddess of the land and thus mother of its ruler, the pharaoh. Pharaohs are often depicted sitting in the lap of Isis and being suckled by her.

J

Jack-in-the-Green   Traditional May Day character, played by a man inside a wood or basketwork frame covered with foliage and flowers so that he looks like a walking and dancing bush. The Jack seems to have been quite localised around the London, Oxfordshire and Buckinghamshire areas, but he can now be seen dancing with the Morris Men in Bristol and other places. He was identified with the Green Man by Lady Raglan in 1939, but there is absolutely no evidence for this.

James I and VI   (King of Scotland 1567–1625; King of England 1603–25) Author of *Demonologie* (1597) and protagonist of the witch craze in England after his succession in 1603. His personal antagonism against witchcraft stemmed from the trial of the North Berwick witches (1590 and 1592) during which Agnes Sampson confessed to raising a storm with a group of witches at Hallowe'en in order to sink James' ship as he travelled back from his marriage in Denmark.

Jarcke, Karl Ernst   Nineteenth century Professor of Criminal Law at the University of Berlin, who made extensive studies of the records of seventeenth century witch trials in Germany, and in 1828 promoted the theory that witchcraft was a surviving remnant of pre-Christian pagan belief.

Jayran, Shan   See *House of the Goddess*.

jewellery   Popular Pagan symbols are to be found fashioned in various types of jewellery, from rings and pendants to belt buckles. The pentagram is most common, followed by the ankh, eye of Horus, goddess figurine, green man, awen, Thor's hammer, runes, winged Isis, or other deity. Stones and resins such as lapis lazuli, amber and jet tend to be favoured, most often set in silver, and may be chosen for adornment in a particular ritual because of their association with a particular deity. In Wicca, female witches always wear a necklace in ritual, and inscribed silver rings are presented by the initiator to the initiate at second degree. See also *garter*.

Jewitches/Jewish Pagans   Jewish Pagans and witches are becoming more noticeable, particularly in North America (New York especially) and amongst women who are comfortable with an identity incorporating both Judaism in Paganism and Paganism (usually in the form of Goddess worship) within Judaism. Some have been dissatisfied with the Pagan focus on Egyptian and Celtic pantheons and have turned to their own cultural traditions for inspiration, claiming that Judaism was not monotheistic in origin and in fact relates more to the history of the Jewish people than to concepts of deity. Starhawk is perhaps the most notable example of a Jewish witch (or 'Jewitch'), happily retaining Jewish traditions within her Paganism, since her Paganism does not require the rejection of her heritage. A public Pagan synagogue was founded in the early 1990s in Minneapolis, Minnesota, called Beit Asherah, 'the house of the Goddess Asherah', and there are now several Jewish Pagan journals including *Di Schmatteh* and *Michtav-Habiru: Newsletter of the Jewish-Pagan Network*.

John Barleycorn   Folk song which tells the story of beer brewing, enacted in some Wiccan covens at Lammas. See also *Corn King*.

Jones, Evan John   A contemporary member with Doreen Valiente of Robert Cochrane's coven in the 1960s, and friend of the Magister, who continued Cochrane's tradition and wrote about it in *Witchcraft: A Tradition Renewed* (Phoenix 1990, with Doreen Valiente). See also *Cochrane, Robert; 1734; Regency*.

Jones, Prudence   A psychotherapist, astrologer, and philosophy super-visor based in Cambridge. Prudence ran the Pagan Federation from 1979–1990, and the Pagan Anti-Defamation League from 1985–1989. In 2000, she was voted President of the Pagan Federation. Her books include *A History of Pagan Europe* (1995, with Nigel Pennick), *Voices from the Circle* (1990, with Caitlín Matthews), *Creative Astrology* (1991), and *The Path to the Centre* (1988).

Jung, C.G. (1875–1961) Swiss psychiatrist who began his career with Sigmund Freud but broke away from him after challenging the latter's concentration on sex. Jung's theory of the collective unconscious and his use of the term archetype have been highly influential on some branches of Paganism, including Wicca. Between 1912 and 1926, Jung studied gnosticism and early Christianity, finding in them a prototype of depth psychology. He believed that, as a result of western culture suppressing gnostic concepts, Christianity had suffered. He looked for ways to reintroduce gnostic ideas into modern culture, and believed alchemy was the right vehicle. The first codex of the Nag Hammadi library found in 1945 was purchased and given to Jung on his eightieth birthday, and is called the Codex Jung.

K

Kabbalah ('to receive' or 'to accept') Often translated as 'tradition', the kabbalah is the Jewish mystical tradition, and in particular relates to a system of esoteric mystical thought and practice which developed during the twelfth and thirteenth centuries, although it dates back to the first century CE. According to legend, God taught the kabbalah to the angels, and it was then transmitted from Adam to Noah, then Abraham, then Moses, who passed it on to seventy elders and encoded it in the first four books of the Pentateuch. The most famous book on the kabbalah is the *Zohar*, or *Book of Splendour*, written in the second century CE, which contains mystical commentary on the Pentateuch. By the mid thirteenth century, kabbalah had developed to include practical techniques such as meditation and recitation of the names of God in order to reach ecstasy. Refugees from the expulsion of the Jews from Spain in 1492 brought the Jewish kabbalah to Florence, where it was blended with Hermeticism by Giovanni Pico della Mirandola who, along with Ficino, was one of the founders of Italian Renaissance Hermetism, or the hermetic-cabalist tradition. During the Renaissance, alchemists and magicians used the kabbalah in esoteric ritual, and it was later harmonised with Christian doctrine. The kabbalah has been very influential on western magic, particularly the Golden Dawn, Aleister Crowley and Dion Fortune, and is popular today in some Pagan traditions. Other spellings include cabbala, qabala, kabbala, all of which derive from the Hebrew root 'kbl'.

Kabbalistic Tree of Life   A glyph showing the emanations of the divine, which are ten in number and form ten sephiroth. The paths between the sephiroth can be travelled through meditations, rituals and incantations, and the tree of life is thus symbolic of the entire universe and its patterns of interaction.

Kali   ('the black one') Often called Kali-Ma ('mother'). She is the most wrathful form of the goddess in Hinduism, representing the destructive aspect of nature and requiring human sacrifice according to some sects. She is perhaps the only Hindu deity to have become popular in Paganism.

karma   ('action', 'deed') Another notion used by Pagans, drawing on Hindu and Buddhist influence. Karma operates as a natural law of cosmic balance and retribution whereby humans reap what their actions sow throughout successive lives. Brahmanical karma tends towards the idea that people exist as they do because of their actions in a past life, whilst Buddhism stresses the ethical and prospective idea of acquiring good karma so that future rebirths will be better.

Karnayna   Name used for the Hornèd God by Alex Sanders, still used by some Alexandrian covens. It means 'Hornèd', and was used to describe Alexander the Great.

Kelly, Aidan   Modern American writer on witchcraft, founder of the New Reformed Orthodox Order of the Golden Dawn, and researcher into the origins of modern Wicca published as *Crafting the Art of Magic* (1991). He reconverted to Catholicism in 1995.

kether   ('crown') The first emanation of the supreme being on the Kabbalistic Tree of Life, perceived as the crown on the head of Adam Kadmon, the primal man. It is also called 'ayin', or 'nothing', since nothing can be known of it – it is God in his primal state, from which everything else flows, the root of all roots. It makes up the supernal triangle along with Binah and Chokmah.

Key of Solomon   A famous magical grimoire or book of spells, attributed to the biblical King Solomon.

Kibbo Kift Kindred   British Pagan organisation developed from the Scout Movement, founded in the early 1920s by John Hargrave, drawing on Anglo-Saxon traditions, Rosicrucianism, and Native American shamanism through which it aimed to restore to urban people the values of the natural world. It observed four Anglo-Saxon festivals in the year, and was open to adults over the age of eighteen. It folded once Hargrave lost interest, but the Woodcraft Folk developed from it. See also *Woodcraft Chivalry, Order of*.

Kingsford, Anna (1846–1888) Occultist and founder of the Hermetic Society. Married to an Anglican clergyman but converted to Catholicism in 1870, and practised as a Doctor of Medicine in London. Her work inspired Dion Fortune. See also *Hermetic Society*.

Kings of the Elements See *Elemental Lords*.

Kipling, Rudyard (1865–1936) English novelist, poet, and story writer who was born in India and set many of his writings in the India of the Raj, epitomizing the British colonial spirit. Awarded the Nobel Prize for Literature in 1907. The penultimate verse of 'A Tree Song' from *Puck of Pook's Hill* (1906) was adopted wholesale by Gerald Gardner for his Beltane/May Eve ritual in the Book of Shadows. Some of Kipling's writings which express clearly the themes of the land and the people as one, folk customs as representatives of old fertility religions, mythology, and the power of flora and fauna have made his poetry popular among some Pagans and were certainly an influence on Gardner.

kiss An important symbol in Wicca, opposite of the scourge, represented on the pentacle by an 'S' (the scourge is represented by '$'). It is regarded as a symbol of the discipline of love, which provides the space in which people can feel safe enough to question themselves calmly and grow into who they are. Maintaining love come what may is believed to be just as difficult as wielding the scourge properly and effectively. The free-flowing quality of the symbol denotes an endless outpouring, as opposed to the controlling line of the scourge.

Knight, Gareth Modern occultist and magician, head of the Western Mysteries groups and the founder of the Companions of Greystone. He trained with the Society of the Inner Light from 1953, leaving in 1965 to develop his own work and returning in 1998. His books include *A Practical Guide to Qabalistic Symbolism* (1965), *The Practice of Ritual Magic* (1976) and *The Rose Cross and the Goddess* (1985). Recently, he has edited Dion Fortune's previously unpublished work and conducted research in the Society's archives to produce *Dion Fortune and the Inner Light* (2000).

knot magic   Most popularly in history knots were used by witches to control the winds, which they would sell to sailors. Knots are also used to symbolise the release of energy in spells, or to bind energy. See also *witches' ladder*.

Kore   ('maiden') Another name for Persephone.

Kundalini   ('the coiled one') A term borrowed from Hindu tantra and popular among groups that make use of chakras. In Hindu tantric sources, Kundalini is the name of a goddess who has the form of a serpent. She is considered to be a pool of raw energy, depicted as a serpent coiled at the base of the spine, which when activated rises up the spine and awakens six chakras or spiritual centres until it reaches the thousand-petalled lotus at the crown of the skull, the point at which the universe and the individual meet.

L

Lammas   (Anglo Saxon, 'loaf-mass') One of the four Greater Sabbats of the Wheel of the Year, Lammas celebrates the first harvest at the beginning of August, the cutting of the corn from which bread is made. The God is cut down by the sickle of the Goddess, his blood spilt upon the land to ensure the return of fertility the following year, giving his life that life might continue. It is considered a time for letting go, giving things up in order to move forward, for the God does not find death, but new life in the realm of the Gods, leaving behind the light of the sun and entering into darkness. Until Lammas, he has been the Lord of Light and life, developing in the conscious world. At Lammas, he begins the transformation into Dark Lord of Death, opening himself to the realm of the unconscious. Opposite to Imbolc on the Wheel, Lammas is a different kind of initiation, into new life of a different order – the God has entered the heroic quest. Lammas is also called Lughnasadh (Irish, 'gathering of Lugh'). See also *Lugh*.

Laws of Witchcraft   One hundred and sixty one laws compiled by Gerald Gardner in archaic language which he claimed were ancient but which he added to his Book of Shadows in the 1950s. They are at times blatantly sexist, particularly in their insistence on the retirement of the High Priestess once she has lost her youth and beauty! Always controversial, the laws led to a split within Gardner's coven in 1957, with Doreen Valiente leading a breakaway section. Never given much credence, some Wiccans have now thrown out the laws whilst others retain them in the Book of Shadows merely to contribute a sense of the history and development of Wicca.

Leek, Sybil (d. 1992) Born Angela Carter in Staffordshire, Sybil Leek was a prominent British hereditary witch in the 1960s and 1970s who founded the Witchcraft Research Association in February 1964 to provide a forum in which Wiccans could settle their differences and reclaim their own history. She was forced to resign as president by July of that year because she had been popularly linked with acts of ritualised vandalism in Sussex. Leek emigrated to the United States, where she spent the rest of her life. She wrote *Diary of a Witch* and *The Complete Art of Witchcraft*. She was never initiated as a Wiccan, and her books enabled covens to spring up which were not based on Gardnerian rules. Her chief deities were Diana and Faunus. She lived for a time with gypsies in the New Forest, and ran an antique shop in a Hampshire village until unwanted tourist attention forced her to sell up. At a time when Wicca and black magic were synonymous in the public mind, Leek believed Aleister Crowley to be a great spiritualist who was ahead of his time and unfairly labelled 'evil', and even claimed to have been trained by him.

Legend of the Goddess A light-hearted mystery play enacted in Gardnerian and Alexandrian covens, based loosely on the classical Greek myth of Persephone's descent to the underworld to become the bride of Hades, itself based on an older Sumerian myth in which Inanna the Queen of Heaven descends to the underworld to challenge its queen, Ereshkigal. The priestess playing the part of the goddess is dressed in seven veils to represent the seven emblems of power which are stripped from Inanna/Ishtar as she passes through the seven portals of the underworld. She is finally bound and led before the altar of the Hornèd God (who replaces Hades), who scourges her before her emblems of power are returned.

Leland, Charles Godfrey (1824–1903) American folklorist and a major influence on the development of Wiccan and Paganism. Leland wrote over fifty books, but it is his last, *Aradia or the Gospel of the Witches* (1899) which has been most influential. Leland travelled extensively in his search for lore, and in Italy in 1866 met a witch called Maddalena who helped with his researches into Italian folklore. After twenty years, in 1886, she confided to him that she knew the location of a manuscript containing details of the origin of Italian witchcraft. However, she never produced the manuscript but instead passed to Leland handcopied sections of the original in 1897. It is thus unclear whether Leland faked the whole of *Aradia*, whether Maddalena was a fraud, or whether Leland interpreted her revelations to fit the ideas of Jules Michelet, whose *La Sorciere* (1862) was a great influence on his *Aradia*. His claim to have discovered the existence of a continuing thread of Italian witchcraft from pre-medieval times therefore remains unsubstantiated.

Lemegeton   Medieval text also known as the *Lesser Key of Solomon*, the earliest copy being in French and dating from the seventeenth century. It contains lists of demons, along with their offices and the rituals needed for their invocation. Divided into four sections, only the *Goetia*, which contains rituals for the conjuration of seventy two demons including Lucifer, Ashtaroth and Bel, is in print.

Lesser Sabbats   The winter and summer solstices and spring and autumn equinoxes.

Lévi, Eliphas Zahed   (1810–1875) Born Alphonse Louis Constant, Lévi was a French priest, defrocked because of his political opinions and failure to keep his vow of celibacy, who became an occultist and magician. Largely responsible for the occult revival in the twentieth century, Lévi wrote his treatise *Dogme et Rituel de la Haute Magie* in 1855 and attempted to create a unified magical system of occult knowledge. His system was adopted by the Golden Dawn, and his works, including *Dogme, Histoire de la Magie* (1860), and *La Clef des Grands Mystères* (1861), were translated into English by A. E. Waite, a prominent Golden Dawn member, and are still in print.

ley lines   Alignments which cover the English landscape linking ancient sacred sites, often dotted with man-made structures such as barrows, cairns, stone circles, wells, and churches. The existence of ley lines was first put forward by Alfred Watkins in *The Old Straight Track* in 1925, in which it was proposed that the lines were used as navigation routes between communities by ancient peoples. Perhaps the most famous is the intersection of lines at Glastonbury, one of which runs from Canterbury Cathedral, through Stonehenge, to Glastonbury Abbey, the second of which runs from St Michael's Mount in Cornwall to Avebury stone circle via Glastonbury Tor. They are regarded as paths of energy emanating from the earth, and some believe that these energies can be tapped and may have magical properties.

libation   Wine and cakes scattered on the earth as thanks to the Goddess.

Liber Al Vel Legis   See *Book of the Law*.

Liddell, E. W.   Commonly known as 'Bill', Liddell is an English occultist living in New Zealand who submitted a series of papers to the journals *The Wiccan* and *The Cauldron* between 1974 and 1977 under the name 'Lugh', in which he claimed to be a middle-man for a group of anonymous traditional and hereditary witches in East Anglia. These witches allegedly belonged to the nine covens of cunning-man George Pickingill, from Canewdon in Essex. The correspondence was collected in a single volume co-authored by Liddell and Mike Howard and published as *The Pickingill Papers* in 1994. Liddell's claims have been treated with suspicion since they are almost wholly unsubstantiated and in some cases at odds with known fact, and in 1996 Liddell retracted many of his claims, which are now accepted as fraudulent.

life force   To some Pagans, the divine is perceived as the life force of the universe rather than anthropomorphised into gods and goddesses.

Lilith   In Jewish mythology, Lilith was Adam's first wife who stormed out of the Garden of Eden after refusing to submit to Adam; she is also a Jewish demon, inhabitor of the lunar sphere of Yesod in the mystical system of the kabbalah.

lineage   'Family tree' of initiation in Wicca, going back to either Gardner or Sanders. Particularly important in American witchcraft where initiates are deemed genuine only if they have a certificate tracing their lineage.

Litha   Alternative name for Midsummer, popularised by Starhawk and used almost exclusively in North America, probably appropriated from Tolkein's use of the word for the hobbit summer festival in *The Lord of the Rings*. It is the Anglo-Saxon name for the double month of the summer in the early English calendar, covering the Roman June and July, rather than the name for the solstice festival.

Loki   Trickster/shaman god in Norse mythology.

Lucifer   ('bringer of light') Italian deity assimilated with Pan and thus with the Christian concept of Satan. Brother of Diana, with whom she had an incestuous relationship the result of which was Aradia. In some Gnostic texts, Lucifer is the first born son of God, and thus divine. Also associated with the morning star and the dawn.

Lugh   An Irish Celtic god of the light, who had the power of shape-changing and was armed with a huge spear and sling, both of which were magical. He may have been adopted as a deity in Roman Britain and there is some evidence for this in place names such as Luguvalium (Carlisle). He gives his name to Lughnasadh, the alternative name for the festival of Lammas.

Lughnasadh   Celtic name for 1st August, the Anglo-Saxon Lammas.

M

Mabinogion   The main repository in verse of Welsh Celtic oral tradition, the *Four Branches of the Mabinogi* make up part of the thirteenth century *Red Book of Hergest. The Mabinogion* contains a great deal of Celtic mythology, but only one of its mythological figures, Mabon ('Divine Youth'), son of Modron, is to be found in inscriptions and place names (in the Romano-Celtic form, Maponus). Robert Graves suggested that Mabinogion means either 'juvenile romances' or 'tales of the son of a virgin mother'. Lady Charlotte Guest's translation of 1848 is the best-known modern edition.

Mabon   ('divine youth') Son of Modron, in Welsh mythology. In North America, an alternative name for the Autumn Equinox. See also *Mabinogion*.

macrocosm   The universe. The reflection of the macrocosm in the microcosm is a key Hermetic principal embedded within the magic and philosophy of the Western Esoteric Tradition and thence transferred to Wicca.

Maeve/Mab   Queen of the Fairies in English tradition. Her name may derive from the Irish goddess queen Medb, but mab is the midwife of the fairies and *mab* in Welsh means baby.

magic   Important in many types of Paganism, the practice of which is by no means a requisite for being Pagan. The difficulty in characterising Wicca and Paganism as religions has been exacerbated by the portrayal of magic as a contra-religious instrumental means of control rather than as a spiritual discipline which may be a constitutive part of group religious practice. Magic in Paganism is understood in the same way as it was portrayed in the Renaissance: it is not set in opposition to religion, but rather is an important element of spiritual growth towards the mystical attainment of gnosis, with any short-term pragmatic goals being secondary to this end result. In Paganism, magic is as much a group practice as individual, and forms an integral part of religion.

Magic tends to fall into three types. The first of these can be termed 'lesser', 'natural', or 'horizontal' magic, and includes traditional concepts associated with witchcraft, for example chants, dances, and poppets. These isolated, specific spells may be performed separately from ritual or at the end of ritual, and tend to be time and place specific, immediate rather than continuous, goal orientated and pragmatic, for example a job spell. In this sense, magic is partly concerned with specific, concrete problems and is thus distinct from religious concerns with the fundamental issues of human existence.

The second magic could be termed 'higher', 'ritual' or 'vertical' magic, or ceremonial magic. This type of magic tends to be performed as part of ritual (e.g. a kabbalistic ritual might be used to empower planetary talismans) and integrated into a whole system of correspondences. Though goal oriented, 'vertical' magic is less immediate and specific than 'low' magic, tending towards the sequential and processual, magic performed as part of ongoing ritual continuity. This 'high' magic can be practised separately from any particular religious belief system although, in Paganism, it tends to be integrated within both a religious and magical worldview.

The third magic is the magic of transmutation, the stripping away of layers and forging of the 'True Will' or pure self. It can be termed the 'greater magic' or 'spiritual alchemy', and is both 'vertical' and 'horizontal' in nature, integrated into both ritual and the everyday world. This magic is journey-oriented, relating to an ongoing process of spiritual and personal growth which is experiential, holistic and non-specific, not limited (to this life) but perceived as an eternal process. The means by which this is done is not the specificity of the spell or defined piece of magic, but the greater magic which is forged within the ritual setting and which occurs as a gradual process marked by initiation and the sequence of rituals which make up the Wheel of the Year. It is not, therefore, measurable scientifically as an effect brought about by a cause, as spellcraft may be, but rather by the noticeable experience of transmutation. The efficacy of the greater magic, the Great Work, can only be measured in incomplete stages, for it is believed to take many lifetimes to come to fruition, or what Jung has termed individuation.

magic squares   Numbers arranged in a square that add up to the same sum in all directions. Used in kabbalistic magic for amulets, talismans, and to compose names of power.

magical weapons   See *working tools*.

magician   A person practising the arts of magic. The term derives from the Greek *mageia*, the Latin *magia*, and the French *magique*. The Greek *magos* specifically defines the astrologers who accompanied the Persian army of Xerxes when they invaded Greece.

maiden   Youthful aspect of the triple goddess, represented in varying pantheons as Artemis, Diana, Astarte, Rhiannon. Also the name given to the deputy of the High Priestess in some covens. In Alexandrian and Gardnerian covens, the maiden will usually be a second degree initiate. In other traditions which do not have three degrees of initiation, the couple running the coven will often be assisted by the Maiden as deputy to the Lady, or High Priestess, and a Summoner who is deputy to the Master, or High Priest.

malkuth   ('the kingdom', 'the bride') 10th sephiroth on the kabbalistic tree of life, also called Shekhinah, representative of God immanent in the world.

Malleus Maleficarum   ('*The Hammer Against Witchcraft*') Compiled in 1486 by the German inquisitor Heinrich Institoris and the Dominican Jakob Sprenger. It was one of the most influential early printed books, and was endorsed by Pope Innocent VIII and prefaced by his papal bull of 1484. The *Malleus* listed the essential features of witchcraft according to the Catholic Church, identified the majority of witches as women, and catalogued their ability to change shape, levitate, and prepare magical potions and ointments. It was published in fourteen editions by 1520, but only appeared in an English translation in recent times.

Man in Black   Character mentioned in various English witch trials, regarded as the devil, but transposed in Murray's accounts to being the local head of the witchcraft cult.

maniblot   Full moon ceremony in Heathenism.

Mathers, Moina   (1865–1928) Born Mina Bergson, sister of the famous philosopher Henry Bergson, Moina contracted a celibate marriage with S. L. MacGregor Mathers after being introduced to him by Annie Horniman, her friend from the Slade School of Fine Art where Moina had studied from the age of 15, winning a scholarship to continue her studies in 1883 and gaining her certificate in 1886. Initiated into the Golden Dawn in 1888, she took the magical motto *Vestigia Nulla Retrorsum* ('never to retrace my steps'). Whilst Mathers headed the Order of the Golden Dawn, it was Moina who channelled the rituals, drew and painted psychically for the Temple, and generally had contact with the inner realms necessary to maintain the Order's momentum. From 1898 onwards Moina and Mathers performed publicly the Rites of Isis in Paris in order to restore the Egyptian Mysteries. Through an article by Frederic Lee, 'Isis Worship in Paris', written in 1899, Moina was able to offer her opinion on women's role in religion, expounding the importance of the priestess who is at the root of all ancient beliefs, for woman is the magician born of Nature. After Mathers' death in 1918, Moina headed a breakaway section of the Golden Dawn, the Alpha et Omega Order, in partnership with J. W. Brodie-Innes. Dion Fortune was initiated into the AO as a neophyte in 1919, before founding her Fraternity of the Inner Light in 1922. Moina later became strongly critical of Fortune for betraying the inner secrets of the Order, and Fortune claimed that she had suffered a psychic attack from Moina.

Mathers, Samuel MacGregor   (1854–1918) One of the most influential modern magicians and occultists, Mathers became a Freemason in 1877 and was initiated as a Rosicrucian before becoming one of the three founder members of the Hermetic Order of the Golden Dawn in 1887. His flair for ritual led to him being delegated the one to devise the rituals based on the cipher manuscripts found by Westcott, to which he added an Egyptian element. In 1891 he went to Paris where he claimed to have received the ritual details from a high adept for the establishment of the Second Order of the Golden Dawn. He moved to Paris permanently in 1894, and continued to be financed by Annie Horniman until she lost patience in 1896. Mathers was the Supreme Chief of the Golden Dawn, but became steadily more autocratic and preoccupied with the darker aspects of magic, partly under the influence of Aleister Crowley, until he was forced from office in 1900. He was obsessed by the ancient Egyptian tradition and formulated the Rites of Isis. He was regarded as one of the main contenders, with Aleister Crowley, for the role of chief magician in

Europe. He adopted various pseudonyms, including S'Rhioghail Mo Dhream and Deo Duce Comite Ferro. He was responsible for the translation into English of several key medieval magical texts, including the *Key of Solomon*, the *Lesser Key of Solomon*, the *Kabbalah Denudata* (Kabbalah Unveiled) and *The Sacred Magic of AbraMelin the Mage*.

matriarchy   A society ruled by women, usually also matrilineal. The importance of the female – as woman and as divine – cannot be underestimated in Paganism, but matriarchy has been of particular importance in feminist witchcraft and goddess spirituality. See also *myth of matriarchy*.

Matthews, John and Caitlín   Prominent figures in Paganism and prolific authors who have between them written over eighty books on the subject of the Western Mystery Traditions, Arthurian myth and lore, and Celticism. Caitlín is also a singer and harpist who runs workshops and offers shamanic counselling and soul retrieval. Her books include *Sophia, Goddess of Wisdom* (1991), *Voices of the Goddess* (1990), *Elements of the Goddess* (1989), and *Elements of the Celtic Tradition* (1989). John is an explorer of Arthurian traditions, and gives lectures and runs workshops in Britain, Europe and America. His books include *King Arthur's Britain* (2001), *The Celtic Shaman* (1991), *Glastonbury Reader* (1991), and *Gawain Knight of the Goddess* (1990). He is currently working on an *Encyclopaedia of Celtic Myth and Legend* (2002). Their jointly-authored books include *The Western Way vols. 1 and 2* (1985; 1986), *Ladies of the Lake* (1992), and *The Encyclopaedia of Celtic Wisdom* (2001).

McFarland, Morgan   One of the founders, along with Mark Roberts, of the witchcraft tradition which eventually became known as Dianic. See also *Dianic witchcraft*.

measure   In Wicca, towards the end of the first degree initiation ritual, the initiand's measure is taken. Using thread, measurements are taken round the head, chest, groin and the length of the body. These are the traditional measurements for the winding sheet and coffin, and are considered to be of great psycho-spiritual and magical importance. The measure is kept by the initiators as a symbolic reminder of their responsibility towards the initiate, and of the initiate's responsibility to the coven and to Wicca. The measure is usually returned to the initiate after the Third Degree initiation, when the initiate is regarded as fully independent and responsible for him- or herself.

Medea (1)   High Priestess of the coven in Derbyshire, who initiated Alex Sanders to first degree on 9th March 1963 after he had been introduced to her by Pat Kopanski, originally a member of Pat and Arnold Crowther's coven in Sheffield. Kopanski was given second degree in Medea's coven, but the death of Medea's husband led her to retire from witchcraft and move away.

Medea (2)   High Priestess of Hecate and powerful witch in Greek mythology, who used her craft to help Jason obtain the Golden Fleece. She has power over animals, travels widely through the night air to gather the ingredients for her cauldron, has both esoteric and worldly knowledge, and is fearless, going out alone into the woods at night, all motifs associated with witchcraft.

meditation   Usually an active process within Paganism where meditation is used for the purpose of visualising in order to train the mind to hold images and thus to facilitate magical work, inner development, and pathworkings.

menstruation   Just as the female is celebrated within Paganism, so menstruation is not taboo. Rites of passage for young girls at the onset of menarche are becoming more and more popular, as are rituals to aid the transition brought about by the onset of the menopause.

Merlin   Variously regarded as the arch Druid, magician, or wizard of King Arthur's court, Merlin is closely associated with the land of Britain.

Michelet, Jules   (1798–1874) French historian who wrote a book portraying witchcraft as a protest against unjust social order, called *La Sorcière,* published in 1862. Charles Leland was influenced by Michelet, and both emphasised a political and class struggle in which witch-cults were deployed, using spells and potions against the oppressive ruling classes in a democratic spirit, as well as portraying women as priestesses in control of the religion. The contemporary historian Ronald Hutton has suggested that the commercial success of *La Sorcière* indicates that Wicca was a religion waiting to be re-enacted. Michelet's ideas have been influential in the modern Pagan revival.

microcosm   Miniature representation of the universe; mankind as a reflection of the universe. The world of manifestation or the 'real world'.

Midgard   In Scandinavian mythology, the region of the earth, inhabited by humans and encircled by the sea. The Midgard serpent is a monstrous serpent, offspring of Loki thrown into the sea by Odin where, with its tail in its mouth, it encircled the earth.

Midsummer   One of the four lesser sabbats, also known as the Summer Solstice and, in the USA, as Litha. The God is called by the Goddess to take responsibility for the land and the people, as well as her and their son. As the sun reaches its zenith, the God is crowned as a king and can no longer roam wild and free in the greenwood. His heart is heavy, however, for by taking the kingship he sees already the sacrifice he must make at Lammas. As the Sun King, he has become conscious of himself and those who depend on him, and also of his mortality. He has reached the zenith of his power in this world, and there is no upward path – from now on he will weaken, just as the sun must weaken as the days grow shorter. Issues of power are relevant to this festival, and the Midsummer ritual is sometimes used to help Pagans come to terms with their own power – when to use it, and when to let it go.

Midwinter   See *Yule*.

Mighty Ones   See *Elemental Kings/Lords*.

Milton Keynes   Buckinghamshire town allegedly constructed according to pagan geomagnetic lines, with its central highway, Midsummer Boulevard, aligned to the sunrise of the summer solstice and its many roundabouts modelled on ancient harvest hills. Many of its roads are named after sacred Celtic sites and there were even plans to construct a replica of Stonehenge, though these were abandoned. Milton Keynes witches made legal history when they were granted the use of public land for the purpose of holding sabbats. However, since the license was hedged with contingencies such as the necessity for a photographic record of all people planning to use the land, along with their athames, and no more than twenty people were allowed to use the land at any one time, it was relinquished after only one year. Nevertheless, the witches felt that an important principle had been upheld.

Minor Arcana   Organisation for Pagan teenagers, founded by Matthew Hannam in the UK in 1998, which folded in 2001.

Mirandola, Giovanni Pico Della   (1463–1494) Italian humanist who used the kabbalah to support Christian theology, earning him the condemnation of Pope Innocent VIII. He was forced to seek the protection of Lorenzo de Medici in Florence. Mirandola blended the Jewish Kabbalah with neo-Alexandrian Hermeticism and is considered, along with Ficino, to be one of the founders of Italian Renaissance Hermetism. In 1486 Pico della Mirandola offered to prove in public debate in Rome that his nine hundred theses drawn from all philosophies were reconcilable with one another. Unfortunately, the debate never took place.

Mithras/Mithraism   Ancient Indian and Persian god of law and justice, a supporter of Ahura Mazda, the great god of order and light, worshipped in Hinduism, Zoroastrianism and Manichaeism, but most well known as a Roman cult. No texts written by any Mithraists have survived, so facts have to be gleaned from outside observers, usually Christian, who were often biased or ignorant; however, archaeology and inscriptions do give some clue to the beliefs of the cult. The earliest reference to the Roman Mithras is by the poet Statius, who died in 96 CE; the earliest known temples were built in the mid-second century, and building continued until the fifth century. The Roman Empire facilitated the spread of the Mithraism as a mystery cult throughout Europe, and temples have been found as far apart as Wales and Egypt, though the greatest concentration of temples is in Rome itself and along the Danube and Rhine valleys. The soldiers of the Roman army made up the greatest number of followers, although traders and officials were also members of the cult. Women were excluded from the cult.

Each community of believers was divided into seven degrees of initiation – Raven, Bride, Soldier, Lion, Persian, Runner of the Sun, and Father. Progression through these grades was thought to reflect the spiritual ascent of the soul away from the material world. Mithraic temples were generally small, built to resemble a cave to reflect the world cave which Mithras had created, with the sky spanning the earth. They believed that Mithras saved his followers through the shedding of eternal blood, and to celebrate this Mithraists shared a feast in imitation of a meal shared by Mithras and Sol (the sun) over the body of the slain bull. Many temples included a relief of Mithras slaying a bull, with plants springing from the blood pouring from the bull's wounds, symbolising regeneration through sacrifice. Mithraism died out in the fourth century, largely because of the spread of Christianity; Christians saw Mithraism as a devilish imitation of what they believed to be the one true religion, and they frequently broke into and destroyed Mithraic temples.

monotheism   Does not exist in any proper sense within Paganism. However, those Pagans who believe all goddesses to be one and the same, and all gods to be one, with one overarching 'divine', are sometimes referred to as monotheists.

Moon   Celestial body associated in Paganism with the goddess, the feminine, menstrual cycle, growth and decay, silver, yesod, night, emotion, psychic abilities, tides, moods and madness (lunacy). It is characterised by three phases – waxing, full and waning – plus the dark of the moon. Pagan gatherings often take place at the full or new moon. See also *correspondences, drawing down the moon, full moon, waning moon, waxing moon, yesod.*

Mor, Barbara   American poet and co-author, with Monica Sjöö, of *The Great Cosmic Mother: Rediscovering the Religion of the Earth* (1987).

Morgan le Fay   The enchantress and half-sister of Arthur in legend, but earlier the mistress of Avalon, where she heals Arthur of his mortal wounds.

Morganwyg, Iolo   Pseudonym of Welsh patriot, Freemason and Unitarian Edward Williams, who was instrumental in reviving Druidry in England and Wales in the 1780s and 90s. A Druidic tradition, he claimed, had survived in Wales through the Bardic system, Welsh language and poetry. His writings were accepted as genuine until the late nineteenth century, when no sources were found upon examination, and Morganwyg was regarded as an imaginative fraud. However, by this time his influence on the revival of Druidry was firmly established and continues to the present.

Morrigan   ('Great Queen') Irish Celtic war goddess, associated with both fertility and death, who mates with the Dagda at Samhain to ensure the prosperity of the land. She is known as the 'sovereignty of Ireland' for she epitomises the sacred nature of the earth. She has a separate form as a triad and can shapeshift from maiden to hag as well as into animals such as deer, ravens and crows.

Mount Haemus Grove   Druid Order founded at Oxford in 1245, which was reconstituted in 1717.

Murray, Margaret Alice   (1863–1963) Born in Calcutta, Murray became a prominent Egyptologist, working under Sir Flinders Petrie at University College London, and an important member of the Folklore

Society. Influenced by Sir James Frazer, Murray's *The Witch Cult in Western Europe* (1921) wove together ideas of rural fertility religion popularised by Frazer, Michelet's witch cult, and folk customs to assert her theory that the witch cult contained the vestigial remnants of a pre-Christian European fertility religion – which Murray called 'Dianic' because it supposedly involved the worship of a two-faced, horned god known to the Romans as Dianus or Janus – and which may have first been developed in Egypt.

Early views of the history of Wicca used Murray's thesis in an attempt to obtain historical legitimisation through claims to an unbroken lineage of witchcraft going back to the Stone Age, presented in terms of an unbroken practice and tradition of witchcraft stemming from the dawn of time. Despite the fact that Murray's theory was never accepted in academic circles, receiving criticism from the time of its publication, her favourable reassessment of witchcraft provided the impetus for a surge of interest in this 'Dianic cult'. In having Murray write the introduction to his *Witchcraft Today* (1954), Gardner perpetuated her theory and made use of her scholastic weight to provide the Craft with a history and tradition which would defy accusations that Gardner had created it *ex nihilo*. During the 1970s, however, historians produced the first specific studies of the Great Witch Hunt and this research overturned Murray's theory. Her sources and her use of them were proved to be defective. Keith Thomas' *Religion and the Decline of Magic* (1971) and Norman Cohn's *Europe's Inner Demons* (1975) exposed Murray's representation of evidence and provided alternative explanations for the Great Witch Hunt.

Murray also wrote *The God of the Witches* (1933) which traced the worship of the pre-Christian Horned God from paleolithic times to the medieval period and explored the rites associated with the dying god, the priest-king who was ritually slain to ensure the continuance of strength and fertility for his land and his people. She suggested that Thomas à Becket, William Rufus, Gilles de Rais, and Joan of Arc were all spiritual leaders whose deaths were ritually imposed. Murray continued with this theme in her 1954 book *The Divine King in England*, in which Gilles de Rais, Joan of Arc, and several English kings were claimed to be the secret leaders of the witch cult until the time came for them to be sacrificed as the witches' god in human form. The ideas set forth in these three books thus became increasingly far-fetched and less convincing, but her *Witch Cult in Western Europe* remained definitive.

Museum of Witchcraft   Originally opened by Cecil Williamson in 1951 on the Isle of Man, where Gerald Gardner was 'resident witch'. After two years Williamson sold the 'Witches Mill' to Gardner and moved his own collection to Windsor. He soon relocated again to Bourton-on-the-Water in Gloucestershire, and then, in 1960, to Boscastle in Cornwall, where it remains. Williamson died just after his 90th birthday in 1999. It is now owned and run by Graham King, who bought the museum when Williamson retired in 1996. The museum houses the world's largest collection of witchcraft related regalia and artefacts, which enables it to put on a large variety of displays covering images of witchcraft, its history, sacred sites, scrying and divination, ceremonial magic, cursing and curses, spells and charms, healing, sea witchcraft, and modern witchcraft. In addition, the museum houses a large collection of press-clippings and has an extensive library. See also *Witchcraft Research Centre; Witches' House Museum.*

mystery religions   Secret religious rites honouring various deities which flourished during the Hellenistic period, such as the Eleusinian Mysteries, Mithraism, Mysteries of Isis, Orphic Mysteries. They involved rites of initiation and spiritual transformation, which Wicca and some forms of contemporary Paganism attempt to emulate.

myth   Of great value to Pagans, who make use of myths from various cultures as a resource for recreating modern versions of ancient pagan rituals, celebrations, and beliefs.

myths of Wicca   Arose within the vacuum of historical knowledge about the witch trials prior to 1970, and as part of the search for a feminist alternative to Wicca's heritage from secret, fraternal, magical societies at the turn of the twentieth century. The myths of Wicca operate as a discourse of descent, creating links to the past, either through associations with the 'burning times' or with a golden age of matriarchy.

myth of matriarchy   The belief among feminist witches that civilisation was once ruled and led by women, based on a matriarchal system, and enjoyed peace and harmony before being overthrown by patriarchal invaders. In some forms of witchcraft matriarchy has become a central controlling image and worldview based on interpretations of historic, prehistoric, and archaeological research. The classic definition of matriarchy was given by J. J. Bachofen as 'rule of the family by the mother, not the father; control of government by women, not men; and the supremacy of a female deity, the moon, not of the male sun'. In *Myth, Religion and Mother Right* (1870), Bachofen argued that society had gone through three evolutionary stages, beginning with general promiscuity, developing into matriarchy and, lastly, becoming patriarchal. After Bachofen, Jane Ellen Harrison, Erich Neumann and Robert Graves promoted the myth in the first half of the twentieth century. From the sphere of feminist politics, the myth of matriarchy and the figure of the Great Goddess entered the realm of feminist spirituality and were used in feminist witchcraft to inform and teach witches, particularly in Dianic, Faery, and Reclaiming witchcraft. Feminist witches regard themselves as reintroducing the world to the Goddess and playing a part in the recovery of humanity from the disastrous turn of events which gave patriarchy the upper hand. Through this use of myth, coupled with literature and techniques from the feminist consciousness movement, feminist witchcraft emphasises empowerment and the move from being a victim to a position of strength, particularly for women.

N

names of power   Secret names of deities, used to invoke power for magical purposes. The strongest name is Tetragrammaton, or YHWH, the Hebrew name of God. See also *incantation*.

Native American Spirituality   A generic term used to denote elements of religious traditions and practices originating within the five hundred or so first nations peoples of North America which have been adopted and adapted by Pagans and New Agers. The term is itself inaccurate, since there is no identifiable 'Native American spirituality'; rather, each tribe had its own religion, language and social practices, varying in belief, practices and influence. Nevertheless, such practices as the use of medicine wheels, power animals, sweatlodges, and vision quests, as well as shamanism have become almost synonymous with the term. Reports of Native American practices and beliefs were compiled by missionaries and anthropologists over the past four centuries, but public interest soared in the 1960s and continues to increase. To indigenous peoples affected by this process, the adoption of such practices by non-Indian people, who remove them from the land to which they are intrinsically linked, has led to controversy and accusations of cultural rape and *homage* based on guilt.

'Aspirational Indians' are perceived as using the 'noble savage' to criticise their own 'civilised' culture. Those who practice Native American techniques, however, often claim that they are more relevant and spiritually satisfying than other traditions available to them. Romanticising the indigenous peoples as 'other', they are held up as more ecologically aware and spiritual, whilst tribes are regarded as the ideal community. Borrowings from Native American cultures have entered some Pagan practices, particularly in North America and noticeably among ecological activist groups, via the Order of Woodcraft Chivalry and associated organisations as well as through first hand contact. See also *Woodcraft Chivalry, Order of*.

Nature Religion   A relatively recent academic construct under which to group a variety of religions, including Paganism, eco-spirituality, and indigenous religions. At present, 'nature religion' is a contested designation, and is itself an emerging field. The current use of the term 'nature religion' stems from Catherine Albanese's usage in her book *Nature Religion in America: From the Algonkian Indians to the New Age* (1990). Albanese defined nature religion as beliefs, behaviours and values which make nature a 'symbolic centre'. Whilst recognising the value of the construct in bringing to light the diversity of religious practices which do take nature as a symbolic referent, Albanese's term has been criticised as too broad to be of practical use. Some academics suggest instead that phrases such as 'the natural dimension of religion', or 'nature influenced religion' be used to distinguish those religions which see nature as important but not sacred, and keeping 'nature religion' exclusively for reference to religions which regard nature as sacred.

Paganism has only recently identified itself closely with the natural world. The growing popular awareness of environmental concerns brought an influx of changes, and awareness that nature religion implies a nature to worship. Yet among 'organised' Pagan traditions such as Wicca and Druidry, few practitioners involve themselves in direct action, and the impact of environmental awareness and activism begs the question as to whether Pagan attitudes towards nature are merely a religious rendering of secular concerns.

necklace   Usually made of amber beads or of alternating amber and jet (the latter traditionally being reserved for third degree high priestesses), a necklace is always worn by female Wiccans in a circle. Amber is organic, a resin rather than a gemstone, and regarded as a goddess stone which represents life; jet, on the other hand, represents death. Necklaces with magical powers appear in mythology, the most famous being the brisinga men of the Norse tradition, a necklace worn by the fertility goddess Freya. 'Brisinga' means 'bright/shining'.

nemeton Sacred grove.

Neo-Paganism (or any other permutation of capitalisation and hyphenation – neo-Paganism, Neo-paganism etc.) A contested term used by some scholars and practitioners to differentiate between ancient and contemporary Paganism, or between broken, or disrupted, religious traditions (e.g. Asatrú, Druidry) and unbroken, or continuous ones (e.g. Hinduism, indigenous peoples such as Australian aborigines or Native Americans). The term is particularly popular in North America and continental Europe, but not in common usage in Britain. It is contested by both academics and practitioners, with practitioners assuming that context makes it apparent whether they are talking about their own contemporary practices or ancient Græco-Roman worship, and regarding the prefix as dangerous because it is easily associated with 'neo-Nazi', or as a trivializing modifier which is disrespectful.

neophyting Name sometimes given to formal, pre-initiation training which might include such things as meditation and visualisation exercises, learning correspondences, reading mythology. In some covens, a neophyte initiation is required, after which neophytes are allowed to observe some rituals.

netzach ('victory') 7th sephiroth on the kabbalistic tree of life, influencing love, beauty and harmony. The right leg of Adam Kadmon.

New Age A term used to describe various religious movements which emerged in the 1960s on the west coast of the USA and spread throughout North America and Europe, with which Paganism is sometimes assimilated. The 1960s saw an upsurge of interest in inner spirituality, especially among those belonging to the counter culture who were seeking to live outside society's norms, rebelling against its organisations and traditions, and trying to find a way of life in which they could encounter and develop their spirituality. Many journeyed to India and the East, in search of gurus, and gurus began to arrive in the USA from India.

However, widespread interest in self-spirituality led also to the development of more organised spiritual paths – in 1962, the most famous and long-lasting British New Age community was established at

Findhorn, which has continued to grow and develop to this day; in the same year, the Esalen Institute was founded in California, and by 1970 it had spawned over 100 centres in the USA. Others include The Church of All Worlds (1962), Silva Mind Control (1966), The Inner Peace Movement (1964), and TM as a popular technique (1968). The counter culture waned in the 1970s, yet the New Age continued and grew, especially in the 1980s and 1990s, becoming more accurately a 'New Age Movement'. Today, there is a huge range of New Age activities on offer, from management seminars in top businesses and industries, to direct action against environmental damage, and including meditation in various forms, many types of alternative healing, massage, aromatherapy, divination, crystals, drumming, chanting, dance and music, past-life regression, how to get rich using mind power, and self-transformation through various methods, to name but a few. The New Age is eclectic, drawing from such sources as world religions, especially the Eastern religions, from physics and cosmology, and from science fiction. Teachings tend to emphasise healing, a balanced life-style and expansion of self awareness through meditation and personal counselling to find the god within.

The New Age movement is characterised by a sense that a new age of spiritual awareness is dawning, for underlying the concept of the New Age is the theory of precession of the equinoxes. This states that, roughly every 2,000 years, a new age of world history begins under the auspices of a different constellation of the zodiac; at present, we are on the verge of the Age of Aquarius (the water bearer) and leaving the Age of Pisces (the dark and light fishes). It is in this sense that the New Age and Paganism are similar, for many Pagans also see the change from Pisces to Aquarius as a sign that spiritual awareness is growing and that spirituality must therefore change. However, in many other ways the two are quite distinct. The New Age is, generally, more utopian, with an emphasis on light and healing, whereas Paganism tends to be more pragmatic, recognising and appreciating darkness and death as part of life's cycle, as well as healing and light. Such distinctions belie a more transcendental attitude within New Age, whereas Paganism regards the divine as immanent. Paganism is less consumer oriented and less mainstream than New Age, although this may change as some forms of Paganism become more acceptable to the mainstream. Both Paganism and the New Age operate across an entire spectrum of attitudes, practices and 'beliefs', and there are thus areas where the two overlap – where there are Pagan New Agers as well as New Age Pagans – just as there are areas where the two are wholly distinct.

New Forest Coven   Coven located in the New Forest, Hampshire, into which Gerald Gardner was allegedly initiated in 1939 and which he claimed was a genuine survival of a witches coven from medieval times. It is also known as the Southern Coven of British Witches. See also *Clutterbuck, Dorothy.*

New Reformed Orthodox Order of the Golden Dawn   Occult group which began as part of a class in ritual at San Francisco State University in 1967, developed into a study group and, by 1969, became a coven based on Gardnerian Wicca, later called the Full Moon Coven. The coven operated by consensus, with no High Priest or High Priestess, and roles rotating among members. NFOOGD dissolved as an organisation in 1976. See also *Kelly, Aidan.*

Nichols, Philip Peter Ross   (1902–1975) Chosen Chief of the Order of Bards, Ovates and Druids from 1964–1975, known within Druidry as 'Nuinn', who produced a definitive account of the history and practice of Druidry in *The Book of Druidry* (1990) the manuscript of which was lost for nine years after his death. Nichols joined the Ancient Druid Order in 1954, but on the death of the Chosen Chief, Robert MacGregor Reid in 1964, the Order split and Nichols became chief of a reconstituted Order, the Order of Bards, Ovates and Druids, which developed the three grades of Bard, Ovate and Druid. The cycle of eight festivals which now make up the Wheel of the Year celebrated by most Pagans was also developed by Nichols, for the ADO had celebrated only the equinoxes and the summer solstice.

nine million, myth of   An exaggerated figure for the number of women said to have been put to death during the great Witch Hunt which until recently constituted a substantial mythic thread. It was computed in the late eighteenth century through the false extrapolation of local records by an antiquarian at Quedlinburg, Germany, and was then repeated by various German historians. The feminist writer Matilda Jocelyn Gage then made use of the number in *Women, Church and State* in 1893 in order to emphasise the crimes of the Church against women. It is from Gage that the number entered Wiccan mythology: the Museum of Witchcraft and Magic on the Isle of Man, owned by Cecil Williamson with Gerald Gardner as 'resident Witch', sported a plaque commemorating the nine million witches who died in the Great Witch Hunt, and Mary Daly's use of the figure in *Gyn/Ecology* (1978) introduced the myth to feminist witches. Estimates of the death toll based on solid evidence were produced in the 1980s, and currently range from 40,000 to 60,000. However, despite the production of such verifiable and academically acceptable figures, the myth retained its hold on feminist witchcraft in particular, acting as a mechanism of legitimisation, reinterpreting the persecution of witches to the Jewish Holocaust of World War II as a holocaust against women.

Norns   Three sisters who sit at the foot of the World Tree, Yggdrasil, in Norse mythology, spinning the wyrd of all the worlds. They are popularly thought of as past, present and future but also interpreted as initiating, becoming, and unfolding.

north   Direction associated with the element of earth, with night, winter, and colours such as black and brown. Its elemental king is Boreas, the Greek name for the north wind. In Wicca, the altar is situated in the North, thought to be the most sacred direction as it is traditionally the home of the Gods, the direction of Caer Arianrhod, the Spiral Castle of the Celtic goddess Arianrhod.

North, Dolores   (d. 1982) London-based Pagan and friend of Gerald Gardner, also known as Madeline Montalban (her pen name for contributions to the occult magazine *Prediction*) and as the Witch of St Giles. She helped Gardner with the typescript for *High Magic's Aid*, and developed a system of inner ceremonial, angelic magic which she called Hermetics. Allegedly retained by the Mountbattens as a psychic aid during World War II.

Norton, Rosaleen   (1917–1970) Australian occult artist and self-taught witch, notorious in the 1950s and 60s for her avant-garde paintings often painted whilst in trance. Melbourne police confiscated some of her art in 1949 on the grounds of obscenity, and although the charges were dismissed her art attracted a great deal of controversy. She was known popularly as the Witch of Kings Cross, the district in Sydney where she lived.

nudity   The practice of ritual nudity in Wicca stems in part from Leland's *Aradia*, picked up by Gerald Gardner, a pioneer naturist who claimed that witches always worked in the nude, even in the impractical climate of the British Isles. Also influential are paintings portraying witches as female and nude, such as *Love's Enchantment (Der Liebeszauber*, Flemish School 1670–80), Grien's *Two Witches* (1480) and Albrecht Dürer's engraving *The Four Witches* (1497), even though there are also numerous representations of the witch in art which, whilst often depicting the witch as female, also paint her fully clothed-Francisco de Goya's *The Spell* (1797–8) and *Witches' Sabbath* (1794–5), for example.

Ritual nudity has been explained with a variety of provenances, including Celtic practices, the Mysteries of Isis and Osiris, ancient Greek and Roman practices of working nude or in loose flowing garments, the Villa of the Mysteries in Pompeii, and tantric worship. To many, being naked, or 'skyclad', allows power to flow from the body unimpeded, and when robes are worn, natural fabrics such as cotton, silk or wool are preferred, as natural fibres are thought to allow magical energy to pass through them. More importantly, entering the circle naked is regarded as a sign of vulnerability and trust, a symbol of emancipation, and a contrast with social norms. Thus, the practice of ritual nudity in Wicca can be regarded as a symbol of freedom, after the Great Charge of the Goddess which exhorts Wiccans to be 'free from slavery, and as a sign that ye be really free, ye shall be naked in your rites'.

Removing the last vestiges of the everyday world through undressing marks a movement from everyday reality into the spiritual realm, and as an inversion of social norms, ritual nudity proclaims a levelling of status, a denial of social distinctions, a uniformity. The body becomes a symbol of trust and intimacy, for those among whom one would be naked is usually a relatively exclusive group and necessitates extra care to keep outsiders away, and is thus linked to inclusion/exclusion and secrecy. On another level, Wiccans going into ritual regard themselves as going before their gods and bearing their souls, represented by being naked. But they not only regard themselves as naked before their gods, but as 'open' to each other and to themselves. In today's body-conscious world, where the media pressure to be ever thinner can be unbearable, it is important to Wiccans that they feel comfortable with their bodies and are accepted by others as they are rather than feeling they would be acceptable if only they could lose half a stone.

This acceptance of the body as sacred can also be interpreted within an esoteric framework. In the Western Esoteric Tradition, the Divine is experienced in the things of earth according to the Hermetic maxim, 'As Above, So Below'. Thus, the body is seen as a magical object, mystically linked to the planets and to the elements of nature. The body is regarded as the most obvious indication of our corporeal existence, as spiritual beings in the physical world. Thus, by working nude, the presence of the physical within the spiritual and sacred space of the circle is made explicit.

numerology   System of divination based on Pythagorean philosophy which taught that the universe was built up from the power of numbers. All words, names and numbers are reducible to a single digit, and these digits have occult correspondences.

O

Oak King   God of the Waxing Year. See also *Holly King*.

oaths   An oath of loyalty and secrecy is taken by each initiate as part of their initiation into Wicca, binding them to protect certain details of the Craft.

occultism   Nineteenth century French development of esotericism, which influenced ritual magic, Theosophy, and spiritualism. It has also been described as the practical side of theoretical esotericism, but this is a rather redundant distinction since esotericism requires personal development and participation rather than theoretical abstraction for its own sake. The term was coined by Eliphas Lévi, who derived it from *philosophia occulta*, used to denote investigations and practices concerned with astrology, magic, alchemy, and the kabbalah. Occultism is now used to denote practices dealing with these occult 'sciences' and to describe the current which emerged with Lévi in the nineteenth century.

occult sciences   Name given to the three sciences of magic, astrology and alchemy legitimated by Hermes Trismegistus in the *Corpus Hermeticum*, rehabilitated by Renaissance hermeticists such as Marsilio Ficino and Cornelius Agrippa as the *occulta philosophia*. Magic here includes the *magia naturalis*, or early natural sciences, as well as the attempt to unify religion and magic, theurgy/white magic, and celestial or astronomical magic. Astrology, as a gnosis of the invisible relationships between the stars and humans as opposed to a mere system of divination, is implicitly magical, and is difficult to distinguish outside of a magical context. Alchemy merges with both astrology and magic, but retains its own character as a spiritual pursuit in which the alchemist is the base metal requiring purification and spiritual regeneration. The occult sciences were revived in the nineteenth century in large part by Eliphas Lévi, who had a profound influence on the Hermetic Order of the Golden Dawn and Theosophy.

Odin/Othin   ('All Father') Norse and Icelandic god, chief among the Aesir sky gods. Principal god of victory in battle and god of the dead, he lives in Valhalla, the Hall of the Noble Slain in Asgard where he rules over an army of warrior spirits, the Valkyries, and heroes slain in battle on earth who will defend the realm of the gods against the Frost Giants on the day of doom, Ragnarok. He is thought to have evolved from a syncretization of the Germanic war gods Woden and Tiwaz, and was the patron of the fierce warrior cult, the beserks. Odin has the attributes of a shaman who shapeshifts and pursues occult knowledge through communication with the dead. He wanders the earth disguised as a traveller, and his symbols are the raven and a spear carved with runes. It was after piercing himself with his spear that Odin hung himself upside down from the world tree Yggdrasil in his desire for knowledge, giving his right eye to the god Mimir to buy permission to drink from the well of knowledge which rises from a spring beneath the roots of the tree.

Odinic Rite   Heathen organisations, focusing strongly on Odinism, north European and English heathen traditions, and runework. There are two Odinic Rites, arising due to a dispute between them. The first has a ruling council, the Court of Gothar, which has nine members and meets each month. It's official ceremonies are written down in *The Book of Blots* (1991), which includes some ceremonies closely related to the eight festivals of the Wheel of the Year celebrated by most Pagans: the Odinic Rite celebrates the solstices and equinoxes, as well as one major festival each month and other significant dates. The blot of Hengest, for example, celebrates English settlement in Britain, whilst in October the reclamation of the White Horse Stone in Kent, said to be the burial place of Horsa, is commemorated. This latter was restored as a site of worship by the Odinic Rite in 1985, and both groups attempted to protect the site from destruction by the Euro-rail link. The first Odinic Rite publishes *The Moot Horn* for members and the magazine *Odinism Today*. The second Odinic Rite is very similar to the first, producing the *Book of Blotar of the Odinic Rite*, which includes developments of Blots found in the *Book of Blots* of the first Odinic Rite, and celebrating festivals on the same dates and under the same names. Both have local groups called Hearths.

Odinist/Odinism   In a general sense, the word used to describe people practising traditions associated with northern deities and their rites, the general term being Asatrú in the USA. More specifically, the term is used to describe a person who works principally with Odin or Woden. See also *Asatrú.*

Odinshof Heathen organisation consisting of groups called Hearths which promotes the teachings of Odin whom it considers to be an enlightened teacher, somewhat akin to the Buddha in Buddhism. It celebrates the eight festivals of the Wheel of the Year as well as full moon rituals (*maniblot*) and, unlike some Heathen groups, has a positive attitude towards mutli-culturalism and homosexuality. Ecology is of particular concern to Odinshof, which has established a Land Guardians scheme which buys woodland and is involved in other areas of ecological activity. Odinshof has two grades of membership: the Odal grade of the novitiate which lasts for at least thirteen lunar months, and the Oak grade. It trains members as *gothar* (priests and priestesses) and is keen to develop the roles of *volva* and *grimsrular.*

Ogg, Gytha (Nanny) One of the three witches who feature in Terry Pratchett's discworld novels. Nanny Ogg is the matriarch of a huge family, who likes a drink and sings raunchy songs!

ogham A series of symbols which allegedly constitute the oldest form of goidelic writing in Celtic Ireland. It is based on the Roman alphabet but is attributed to Ogma, a warrior deity and son of the Dagda. The alphabet is described in detail in Robert Graves' *The White Goddess* (1948), and has also been called the Tree Alphabet since each letter has been associated with a tree. It consists of twenty letters – fifteen consonants and five vowels – in the form of intersecting lines above, below, or cutting through a base line. It has been claimed that this reflects the fingers of one hand placed against the palm of the other, the effect being a proto sign language. The only surviving examples are carved in stone and date from the fourth and fifth centuries BCE, but evidence suggests that ogham was more frequently inscribed on the bark of hazel or aspen wands.

Olcott, Colonel Henry Steel (1832–1907) Co-founder, with Madame Blavatsky, of the Theosophical Society, becoming sole leader after her death, and succeeded by Annie Besant.

Order of Bards, Ovates and Druids Druidic organisation founded by Ross Nichols in 1964 as a breakaway movement from the Ancient Druid

Order. It is an Arthurian Druid order with an emphasis on Celtic mythology and earth mysteries, with elements taken from the Golden Dawn similar to Wicca (elements, 4 quarters etc.). Since 1988, OBOD has run a correspondence course in Druidry, offering readings, tapes and workbooks which facilitate progress through different grades. The Bardic level involves studies of the four elements, the circle of nature, the Sun, the Earth, the calendar, poetry and developing the artistic self. In the ovate grade, students work on healing and divinatory skills and study tree-lore, animals and plants, sacred sites, ley-lines, and Arthurian legend. For Druids, the study of Arthurian and grail myths gains in importance, as well as work on the triple knot and mysteries of the serpent's egg. Druids are also shown how to open and lead a grove. The present Chosen Chief of the Order is Philip Carr-Gomm.

Ordo Templi Orientis   German occult order founded in 1904 by the occultist and Freemason Karl Kellner. Its British branch was headed by Aleister Crowley in the early years of the twentieth century, and spread to the USA where Crowley resided from 1915–1919. Rudolf Steiner also headed a chapter before going on to found the Anthroposophical League. Crowley took over as head of the entire order in 1922, but after his experiments in Sicily at the Abbey of Thelema, which lead to his removal from Italy by Mussolini, the Order was discredited and banned in England in 1923. In 1934, it was also outlawed and disbanded in Germany. Derived from mystical Freemasonry, it was influenced by the writings of French occultist Eliphas Lévi, Indian traditions of tantra and yoga, and myths of the Knights Templar. It is still in existence today, as two main groupings – the Caliphate or English branch of the American O∴T∴O, and the British Typhonian O∴T∴O.

Orphism   Mystery religion of ancient Greece dating from the sixth or seventh century BCE and based on now lost poems attributed to Orpheus emphasising the mixture of good and evil in human nature and the necessity for individuals to rid themselves of the evil part through ritual and moral purification over a series of incarnations. It had declined by the fifth century, but was an important influence on Pindar and Plato.

Osiris   Husband and brother of Isis and posthumous father of Horus, Osiris was an Egyptian god associated with fertility who was murdered by his brother Set and restored to life as ruler of the afterlife. Dead pharaohs were associated with Osiris, the living with Horus.

ovates The middle level in the Druidic system, though in fact in most Druid groups there are no specific groups labelled 'Bard', 'Ovate' or 'Druid', and all are Druids. Ovates have the specific task of listening to the otherworld to discover the wisdom of the future, particularly through tree-lore, ogham, and coelbren. They are also known as healers, using herbalism, homeopathy and therapy, and often facilitate rituals.

Owen, Ruth Wynn Name used by an actress and voice coach who claimed an hereditary family tradition, became involved in the Regency, and founded groups of her own in London and Yorkshire which supposedly worked her own family tradition of Welsh witchcraft which she called Plant Brân. See also *Plant Brân; Regency.*

P

pagan Term derived from the Latin *paganus* used to denote (1) pre- and non-Christian people in the ancient world; (2) non-Christians, often extended to non-Christians, -Jews, and -Muslims, including atheists, hedonists, and agnostics; (3) people of a specific locale, and by extension the religion of that locale; (4) contemporary practitioners of a variety of traditions which draw inspiration from pre-Christian religions as revealed in archaeology, classics, and myth in order to revive and recreate old practices and beliefs in the context of modern day life. Such practices and beliefs tend to include the veneration of nature, reverence of old pagan goddesses and gods and a rejection of patriarchal monotheism. See also *Introduction.*

Pagan Dawn Journal of the Pagan Federation, originally called *The Wiccan* until a change of name was agreed in 1994 in order to reflect the diversity of the Pagan Federation membership and readership of the journal. It is published quarterly.

Pagan Federation Pagan organisation established in 1989 when the Pagan Front was renamed. Three principles were formulated to which Pagans are supposed to adhere: reverence for nature, the Pagan Ethic or

Wiccan Rede, and honouring the divine as both female and male. The Pagan Federation promotes contact between Pagan groups, provides information for seekers, provides practical and effective information on Paganism to members of the public, the media, teachers etc, and works for the rights of Pagans to worship freely and without censure according to Article 18 of the Universal Declaration of Human Rights.

Although Wiccans established the Federation, and every president until 1997 was Wiccan, the growth in Paganism led the Federation to reformulate in order to take account of the new developments. In 1994, the journal of the Pagan Federation was thus changed from *The Wiccan* to *Pagan Dawn* to reflect the Pagan Federation membership. *Pagan Dawn* is published quarterly, and in addition many Pagan Federation Regions publish their own magazines containing contacts, events, and articles. Regions have their own conferences, and there is an annual Pagan Federation conference in London. Other events, either regional or national, are sometimes open to the public or for members only.

Pagan Front   Pagan organisation established by John Score in September 1970, developed from a small-circulation inter-coven newsletter called *The Wiccan*, first published in 1968. It aimed to bring together people from different Pagan religions, to provide information on Paganism to the general public and to counter misconceptions about Pagan religions. Its inaugural meeting was held in London on 1st May 1971, chaired by founder member Doreen Valiente. In 1989 the organisation changed its name to the Pagan Federation.

Paganism   Term variously applied to (1) the pagan religions dominant in the classical ancient world, particularly of Greece and Rome, interest in which was revived in the nineteenth century; (2) the indigenous peoples of Asia, Africa and the Americas; (3) the powerful rural myth of pastoral innocence pre-World War I epitomised in the writings of Walt Whitman and Edward Carpenter; (4) a variety of contemporary traditions and practices which revere nature as sacred, ensouled or alive, draw on pagan religions of the past, use ritual and myth creatively, share a seasonal cycle of festivals, and tend to be polytheistic, pantheistic and/or duotheistic rather than monotheistic, at least to the extent of accepting the divine as both male and female and thus including both gods and goddesses in their pantheons. Contemporary Paganism includes a variety of traditions of witchcraft, initiatory Wicca, Pagan Druidry, Asatrú or Heathenism, Pagan shamanism, and 'non-aligned' Paganism. Some argue that Paganism also includes Hinduism and Shinto.

Pagan Way   Loose organisation which emerged in 1971 in the USA, since existing covens could not accommodate the number of enquiries received from prospective initiates, partly as a result of the publication of Susan Roberts' *Witches USA*. The Pagan Way set out to provide an alternative to an initiatory coven setting, having no formal initiation or requirements for membership, and emphasised the celebration of nature rather than the practice of magic. It continued to exist until about 1980, as Pagan Way groups were formed, teaching materials were used prior to initiation into Wiccan covens, and solitary Pagans found guidance in its mailings. Key figures involved in the Pagan Way included Ed Fitch, Joseph Wilson, and Thomas Giles in the USA, and John Score, Tony Kelly, and leaders of Regency and Plant Brân covens in the UK.

Pan   Greek shepherd god of Arcadia, son of Hermes, perceived as the personification of wild nature. His sudden appearance was believed to cause terror, or 'panic', similar to that of a stampeding flock or herd. Much of his symbolism is phallic, but it was his association with wild nature which led to his revival in the nineteenth century. From the 1870s onwards, Pan as great god of nature became one of the most prevalent ancient images to be drawn upon in art and literature Examples include Arthur Machen's 1894 novel *The Great God Pan*, and H. H. Munro (Saki)'s 'The Music on the Hill' (1911), both of which feature Pan as a central figure, whilst Kenneth Grahame's *The Wind in the Willows* (1907), and J. M. Barrie's 'Peter Pan in Kensington Garden' (1906) made Pan accessible to children. Christian associations of Pan's characteristics (cloven hooves, horns) with their image of the Devil have led to Pan's popularity within occult and Pagan groups being interpreted as a deliberately chosen symbol of opposition to Christianity. But he was also popularised by Dion Fortune in her novel *The Goat Foot God* (1936) in which Pan is called to return to earth and lead humanity 'from darkness unto day', to open 'the door which has no key', 'the door of dreams by which men come to thee'.

Pan Pacific Pagan Alliance: Contact and representative network for Pagans of all paths in Australia and New Zealand, founded c.1990 by British-born Wiccan Julia Phillips.

panentheism   ('everything exists in God') The theory that God is immanent in the universe, but is also transcendent. Different from pantheism, which holds that everything is divine.

pantheism Widespread among Pagans, the divine is considered immanent in the forces and substances of nature, is thus identifiable with nature, and everything is divine. It also refers to the admissibility or toleration of all deities, another deeply-held Pagan value.

Paracelsus (c.1493–1541) Swiss physician born Theophrastus Phillipus Aureolus Bombastus von Hohenheim, who developed a new approach to medicine and philosophy which condemned medical teaching not based on observation and experience. He replaced traditional herbal remedies with chemical remedies, and gave alchemy a wider perspective. Paracelsus regarded illness as having a specific external cause rather than simply being the result of imbalance of humours in the body, and he was famous for rejecting traditional medical theories and procedures in favour of learning from the techniques and practices of folk medicine. Paracelsus disapproved of the notion that the body is controlled by the stars, and some of his medical procedures anticipated modern homeopathy. He was part of the neo-Platonic revival in Northern Europe and had an occult perspective on the world, attempting to unite nature mysticism with Christian dogma and arguing that a ladder of creation from base matter to God existed. He described magic as an art which reveals its highest power and strength through faith, and perceived the entire cosmos as a single entity, the *Diva matrix* or divine womb of the earth mother, thus earning him the label of 'woman worshipper' from the church.

passwords Two traditionally secret, but long-since published passwords for entering the Wiccan circle at first degree initiation are given – 'Perfect Love' and 'Perfect Trust'. The concepts of perfect love and perfect trust are mutually accepted by all Wiccans, and are emphasised by the oaths of secrecy and protection taken at initiation.

pathworking Guided visualisation facilitated by the narration of an imaginary journey, often involving a descent, encounter, dialogue/activity, and return. Sometimes it is done in a group, with one person acting as the narrator and leading the pathworking, but pathworkings are also undertaken alone by those who have developed the skill to use the technique. The purposes of pathworking are many, and include setting the scene for a particular ritual, healing, psychological needs, personal development, overcoming a problem, enhancing psychic awareness and skills such as visualisation, and group bonding.

Pendragon, Arthur Uther Prominent Druid who believes himself to be a reincarnation of King Arthur who is said to lie sleeping until a time of great national emergency. Pendragon claims that this is a time of great spiritual emergency for Britain. He involves himself in a number of Druid gatherings.

Pennick, Nigel Prominent Pagan writer on earth mysteries and sacred landscapes, based in Cambridge.

pentacle Disc of copper, wood or other material representing the earth, engraved with various symbols of Wicca representing the four elements, the God and Goddess, the three degrees of initiation, the eight fold path and, predominantly, the pentagram (part of the third degree symbol). It is regarded as a magical weapon of the element of earth, with its properties of stability and practicality, and thus symbolically acts as a reminder that we are of this earth, magic manifests on earth, the stability needed for effective magic, and that Wiccans must live a normal life which involves taking care of earthly practicalities such as eating, sleeping, shopping etc. One of the working tools of Wicca. See also *working tools*.

pentagram The five-pointed star is a mystical symbol which has been used for thousands of years to symbolise man and the coincidence of microcosm and macrocosm, for it is the image of a human who, standing with arms and legs outstretched, fits it perfectly, as depicted in Leonardo da Vinci's *Proportions of the Human Figure* (c. 1492). Also regarded as the five senses of man, the gateways by which impressions of the outer world reach us. The followers of Pythagoras called it the pentalpha, seeing it formed from five letter As, and it occurs among the emblems of Freemasonry. It is also known as the endless knot, because it can be drawn without lifting the pen from the paper in one continuous line. It is a symbol of the kabbalistic sephiroth Geburah in Jewish mysticism, and in Christianity, when inverted, the pentagram is considered to be a symbol of the devil, but as a representation of the Five Wounds of Christ when upright, for which reason it was painted on the shield of Gawain in Arthurian legend.

The pentagram is the most widespread symbol used in Paganism. Each point of the star represents one of the four elements – earth, air, fire and water – and the fifth the element of aethyr, or spirit, which rules the other four. The symbol represents the subjection of the material world to the spiritual realm or, when inverted as the symbol of the Wiccan second degree initiation, the descent of the spirit into inner depths – the symbol of life but also of the Hornèd God as Lord of Death. The inverse pentagram can also be interpreted as the light of spirit hidden in matter, as well as by the more common popular association of it with the devil or the Goat of Mendes, the two upward points being his horns. As a whole, the pentagram is a symbolic representation of the journey through the three degrees of initiation in Wicca, and has been used to symbolise the Jungian aspects of personality. Apples are regarded as a particularly magical fruit because, when cut across, the form of a pentagram is revealed in the seed pods.

Pentagrams are drawn in the air with the athame or finger and visualised in flaming colours at each of the four quarters when the Elemental Lords are called to the circle. It is also a formal position adopted by the priest or priestess during rituals, when arms and legs are extended to symbolise the star of life.

Pickingill, George   (1816–1909) Cunning man of East Anglia, said to have been leader of the witches in the Essex village of Canewdon and in charge of a circle of nine covens, into several of which both Aleister Crowley (in 1899) and Gerald Gardner were said to have been initiated. Pickingill claimed the title of Hereditary Magister or witch master and allegedly syncretized rites culled from other occult organisations such as the Freemasons and Rosicrucians with some of the more traditional concepts of witchcraft, including coven structure and three degrees of initiation. It is also alleged that people came from far and wide to consult him on occult matters, but none of these claims have been substantiated. See also *Liddell, E. W.*

Plant Brân   Supposed family tradition of Welsh witchcraft founded by the actress and voice-coach Ruth Wynn Owen, who was involved in the Regency, before founding groups of her own in London and Yorkshire to practice Plant Brân. The tradition is very similar to Wicca, using the label Old Religion, venerating a god and a triple goddess, working magic, and celebrating eight seasonal festivals.

polytheism   Belief in or worship of more than one god. Many Pagans are polytheists, some are duotheists, and some could even be said to be monotheists or atheists. They can even be several of these simultaneously. It is difficult to generalise when it comes to Pagans, but perhaps what is true is that the relationship of Pagans with deity is quite different to that of the monotheistic traditions – they embody a different perspective, celebrating diversity, honouring one deity among many, honouring many deities, believing in deity only as a symbol, an archetype, or as completely non-existent, incorporating monotheism into polytheism. See also *pantheism; panentheism.*

poppets   See *fith-fath.*

power   See *energy.*

power animals   Borrowed from Native American traditions and shamanic cultures. Some Pagans believe they have a special and specific relationship with an animal or bird to which they owe honour and allegiance for its help in acting as a spirit guide. Favourite power animals tend to be the powerful or sleek, such as lynx, tiger, panther, buffalo, eagle, hawk etc., but others are less likely and include the hyrax, penguin, puffin, and wombat. Finding one's power animal is often done by means of a guided visualisation or pathworking, sometimes called a 'vision quest', although they are also believed to sometimes make themselves known spontaneously.

Pratchett, Terry   (b. 1948) Author of the Discworld series, which includes extremely astute observations of Pagans in characters such as the witches and wizards, their behaviour towards deities, nature, the occult, magic, and psychology. Not all Pagans warm to this humorous portrayal, but many find the recognition of themselves or their friends in his characters highly amusing. Writing at a time when books on Wicca and on witchcraft are commonplace, Pratchett has been able to blend the new and the old in the witch books of his Discworld series, which star Granny Weatherwax, Nanny Ogg and Magrat Garlick. *Wyrd Sisters* (1988) parodies Shakespeare's *Macbeth*, whilst in *Equal Rites* (1987), Granny Weatherwax defines witchcraft as being about herbs and curses and flying around of nights and generally keeping on the right side of tradition, rather than mixing with goddesses.

priest/priestess   Many Pagan traditions have priests and priestesses, whether they are initiated as such (as in Wicca) or choose to take the titles because it makes sense to them. Some groups give a great deal of training for the priesthood, whilst others require nothing. There tends to be a belief in the 'priesthood of all believers', and as such there is no priestly hierarchy (even in Wicca, High Priestess and High Priest are based on experience) or sacerdotal community. Pagan priests and priestesses are merely recognised as people capable of conducting or participating in ceremonies, rather than having any inherent authority. Some Pagan groups in North America have legal recognition as priests and priestesses by which they are entitled to officiate at weddings, funerals etc. which will be legally recognised. In Heathen groups, priests are called *Gothi* and females *Gythja*.

psychology   Current injected into the development of Paganism by Dion Fortune. Vivianne Crowley, a psychologist who has been a Gardnerian/ Alexandrian Wiccan Priestess for over twenty years, reintroduced Dion Fortune's incorporation of psychology into Wicca. Her book *Wicca* (1989) applies Jungian psychology to the processes of Wicca. This is popular among some covens, but has been heavily criticised by some Pagans as a 'psychologisation of religion' whilst others regard psychology as having nothing whatsoever to do with the occult. It is interesting to note that Neuro-Linguistic Programming became popular among some Wiccans in the closing years of the twentieth century, whilst others have regarded it as no different from what they do in magic anyway.

Pymander   The first of the fifteen treatises of the *Corpus Hermeticum*, which includes a creation myth similar to that in Genesis and tells of the divine mind revealing itself as Pymander to Hermes Trismegistus, giving him instructions, revealing to him the nature of the All and investing him with powers. It was translated into English in 1649 by the hermeticist John Everard despite Isaac Casaubon's discrediting of its pre-Christian origins earlier in the seventeenth century.

Q

qabala   See *kabbalah*.

quarters   The four cardinal directions, marked by candles in ritual and called once the circle has been cast. See also *Elemental Kings/Lords*.

Quest   Journal founded in 1970 and edited by Marian Green since that time. Published quarterly, the journal presents itself as a quest for the magical heritage of the west and contains articles on all aspects of the Western Mystery tradition, natural magic, divination, book reviews, and news of conferences and events. A *Quest* conference is held annually in London.

quintessence   See *Aether*.

R

Ragnarök   (Icelandic, 'twilight of the gods') In Norse mythology, the final battle between the gods and the powers of evil, equivalent to the Germanic *Götterdämmerung*.

Reclaiming   Community for feminist spirituality and counselling founded in 1980 by Starhawk and others in San Francisco, California, largely based on Faery Wicca, feminism, and environmental and political activism. Reclaiming offers classes, counselling, public rituals, witch-camps and workshops in the tradition of Goddess religion, based largely upon reclaiming the image of the witch and empowering women (and men) with the Goddess in order to effect political, environmental and social change. The Reclaiming 'Principles of Unity' explicitly sets out these aims, claiming to 'work for all forms of justice: environmental, social, political, racial, gender and economic. Our feminism includes a radical analysis of power, seeing all systems of oppression as interrelated, rooted in structures of domination and control' (Reclaiming Principles of Unity, September 1998). In the summer of 1998 the first UK Reclaiming 'Witchcamp' was held in Britain.

Regardie, Israel   (1907–1985) English occultist who was Aleister Crowley's secretary between 1928 and 1932. He was initiated into the Stella Matutina in 1934, but left the order after becoming disillusioned with it. He lived most of his life in America, and is most famous for breaking his vows of secrecy by publishing the occult teachings of the Golden Dawn in four volumes between 1937 and 1940, which some blamed for the demise of both of the surviving Golden Dawn splinter groups, the Stella Matutina and the Alpha et Omega. Regardie published many books, including *The Legend of Aleister Crowley* (1930), an overview of the Western Magical Tradition, *The Tree of Life* (1932), and the kabbalistic treatises *A Garden of Pomegranates* (1932) and *The Middle Pillar* (1938).

Regency   London-based witchcraft group founded on Hallowe'en 1966 by friends of Robert Cochrane after the latter's death in 1966. It was named the Regency, according to some, because the human personality is the regent for the divine within; others claim the name was used because the group was formed to continue Cochrane's tradition until his son came of age and could lead it (which he was not willing to do). It took its inspiration from Cochrane's beliefs in the ancient mystic elements of the craft, and proclaimed itself a 'religious society with a central belief in a Goddess as mother and creatrix of all things'. Ruth Wynn Owen, an actress and voice coach who claimed a hereditary family tradition, became involved in the Regency, before founding groups of her own in London and Yorkshire which supposedly worked her own family tradition of Welsh witchcraft which she called Plant Brân. The Regency took the ideas of Cochrane, Wynn Owen, and Robert Graves to produce its rites, was non-hierarchical, and was innovative in its outdoor celebration of seasonal festivals which were open to anyone. See also *1734*.

reincarnation   Many, though by no means all, Pagans have a belief in reincarnation which may take a variety of forms. For some, the soul rests in the Summerlands or at Caer Arianrhod before being reborn. According to the idea of spiritual progression, it may be believed that once souls are advanced enough they are permitted to choose the circumstances of their birth and next life, perhaps with a specific purpose. Souls might eventually reach a state where they do not need to reincarnate or, conversely, reincarnation can be regarded as an unending cycle. Yet another belief is that each soul needs to experience everything, and until it has done so will continue to reincarnate. Death is thus not perceived merely as an ending within Paganism, but the beginning of a new level of existence between incarnations after which the soul will reincarnate. In Wicca, it is hoped that rebirth in the physical plane will be at such a time and place that witches will be able to meet, remember and know each other again.

Rex Nemorensis   ('king of the wood') Title given to Dianus. See also *Cardell, Charles*.

Rhiannon   ('Great Queen') Welsh Celtic goddess who features in the *Mabinogion*, specifically in the *Mabinogi of Pwyll*, Prince of Dyfed. She is associated with fertility, mares, and ravens. She rides a white mare, and has strong associations with the underworld of Annwn and with sorcery.

Ring of Troth   American Odinist group founded by Edred Thorsson in 1987, which functions as a religious institution in which the heritage of the Norse/Germanic religions can be reconstructed. Thorsson laid out the basics of the Ring of Troth in his 1992 book *A Book of Troth*. See also *Asatrú; Asatrú Free Alliance; Rune Gild UK*.

rites of passage   Rites which form part of the exoteric celebrations of Paganism, marking changes in social status, including Wiccanings for the birth of a new child, handfastings, and funeral rites. Initiation rituals can also be termed rites of passage, with the emphasis on spiritual and psychological growth rather than physical maturation or change in social status.

ritual   A significant component of Paganism, deriving for the most part from ceremonial magic via the Hermetic Order of the Golden Dawn, Wicca, and Druidry. The generic framework tends to involve purification through the elements (earth, air, fire, water), casting of the circle or some other form of delineating the sacred space, honouring the four quarters/ invoking Elemental Lords, invoking deity, performing the intent of the ritual, whether it be magic, worship, rite of passage etc., feasting and celebrating, thanking deities, spirit of place, elements for their attendance, banishing the circle. Techniques are used to manipulate the atmosphere (candlelight, music, incense) and the state of consciousness (dance, chants, visualisation, chakras, and fasting). Rather than regarding ritual as a relic of the past, Pagans emphasise ritual as a means of experiential knowing, a way in which the true meaning of their religion can be expressed and experienced. It is used to facilitate awareness of a reality beyond the everyday, where the divine can be experienced, in a sacred space which is perceived to be situated on the threshold between the 'world of men and the realms of the Mighty Ones', a space 'between the worlds', 'a place that is not a place and a time that is not a time'.

Robertson, Olivia   (b.1917) Founder of the Fellowship of Isis in 1976 along with her brother Lawrence Durdin-Robertson and his wife Pamela at Huntingdon Castle, Clonegal, Eire. Involved in spiritualism since childhood, Olivia developed her psychic skills, converting to Goddess worship in 1956, after her brother, an Anglican clergyman, became convinced of the importance of the Mother Goddess. She trained as a medium and healer in London from 1963 to 1974, pursuing her interest in the Egyptian goddess Isis, publishing a theosophical work, *The Call of Isis*, in 1975. Still a very active force within the Fellowship, attending World Parliaments of Religion and travelling widely to Fellowship of Isis conventions, Olivia has also written novels and worked for the Red Cross during World War II.

robes Many Pagans wear special clothes set aside for ritual work, usually made from natural fabrics such as cotton, silk or wool which are thought to allow magical energy to pass through them. Some are simple in design, such as the traditional white hooded robes of the Druids. Others may be more elaborate, such as those used in ceremonial magic which may be specifically chosen according to correspondences appropriate for rituals, or handfasting robes which are made or chosen with as much care as one might choose a wedding dress. Cloaks are also often worn, as well as robes, particularly for outdoor rituals where they serve the pragmatic purpose of keeping practitioners warm. See also *nudity*.

Roebuck US witchcraft coven in Los Angeles run by Ann and Dave Finnin, stemming from the 1734 tradition which derived from Cochrane via Joe Wilson.

Rose of Ruby and Cross of Gold Elite, secretive Second order of the Golden Dawn, with rituals based on the supposed discovery of the Tomb of Christian Rosenkreuz. Its rituals were obtained from a Belgian adept, Dr Thiessen of Liege (*Frater Lux Tenebres*). Known as the 'Vault of the Adepts', the members were known only by secret mottoes.

Rosicrucian Society Also known as the Order of the Rose and Cross and as the Societas Rosicruciana in Anglia (SRIA), the society is an occult organisation founded in England by Robert Wentworth Little aided by W. R. Woodman, F. G. Irwin, and Kenneth MacKenzie, all fellow Freemasons, in 1865. It associated itself with the German Fraternity of the Rosy Cross, allegedly founded in Medieval Europe by Christian Rosenkreuz (an allegorical figure), although the name first appeared in a pamphlet in Cassell, Germany in 1614. Rosicrucianism was popular during the English interregnum, and during the nineteenth century attracted many Freemasons, membership of the SRIA being restricted to Master Masons. Drawing on gnosticism, alchemy, esotericism and theories of reincarnation, members strive for perfection and the attainment of true knowledge or cosmic consciousness over many lifetimes. Woodman and another member, W.W. Westcott, went on to found the Golden Dawn, and Gardner is said to have found the New Forest coven hidden within a Rosicrucian society in Christchurch.

Rune Gild UK   Part of an organisation founded in the USA by Edred Thorsson, and led by Freya Aswynn in the UK. It specialises in the study of the runes, and has three levels of membership in common with old craft Guilds – Apprentice, Fellow/Journeyman, and Master. Beyond these is the Grandmaster, called *Drighting* or *Drighten*. Freya Aswynn is *Drighting*, whilst Edred Thorsson is the highest of the group, the high Grandmaster or *Yrmin Drighten*. The Rune Gild stresses *seidr* and is open to all, rejecting racist attitudes, and has close links with the Ring of Troth.

runes   Discovered by Odin, runes are the most widely used symbols in Asatrú. The runic symbols are thought to be embodiments of truth, and are used for divination, magic, and decoration to honour the gods. Various 'alphabets' of runes are used today, stemming from various roots – Anglo-Saxon, Norwegian and Icelandic.

Russell, George (Æ)   (1867–1935) Irish mystical poet and artist; co-founder, with his friend W. B. Yeats, of the Dublin Hermetic Society in 1885, the purpose of which was to study the western mystical traditions. Russell was its president and held the post until 1933. He was also a member of the reconstituted Dublin Theosophical Society from 1904 to 1933, becoming its president in 1909 when it seceded from the Society, and was deeply involved in Irish nationalism, editing the *The Irish Homestead* from 1905–1923 and the literary and political journal the *Irish Statesman* from 1923–1930. He believed in the pagan Irish deities, and that they would be venerated once again and sought to have Druidic Ireland recognised as one of the world's great ancient civilisations. His pen-name, Æ, was an abbreviation of ÆON, the new aeon which he believed was approaching both for Ireland and globally, as the transition from the Age of Pisces to the Age of Aquarius proceeded. Russell developed his own spiritual system, written in the 1910s in *A Candle of Vision*, which included belief in a single divinity which divided into a Great Father and a Great Mother from whom all gods and goddesses were formed and became independent entities who communicated with humans from the Many Coloured Land.

S

sabbat Traditionally regarded as the meeting to which witches flew for their rituals. The origins of the term come from the identification by early demonologists of witches with Jews, both of which were characterised as the antithesis to Christianity. Montague Summers traces the word from the Phrygian deity Sabazius, patron of licentiousness and worshipped with 'frantic debaucheries'. 'Sabbat' in contemporary Paganism refers to the eight seasonal festivals which are marked with ritual and which together constitute the mythic-ritual cycle known as The Wheel of the Year.

Sabian The name taken by a group of esotericist non-Muslims living in Harran (near the Euphrates) when forced by the Caliph of Baghdad to reveal who they were in 830 CE. Since Islam offered protection to peoples officially recognised in the Koran, they called themselves Sabians, people from Saba (the biblical Sheba), a region of southern Arabia now comprising Yemen. To gain full recognition and protection, they were required to name the book of their sacred scripture, and cited certain texts ascribed to Hermes Trismegistus. Hermeticism thus became the official religion of the Sabians.

sacred marriage See *Great Rite*.

sacred sites Places which Pagans consider sacred vary greatly, but tend to be landmarks from pre-Christian times such as stone circles, barrows, and cairns, tors such as that at Glastonbury, places associated with King Arthur, such as Merlin's Cave at Tintagel and Snowdon, and churches thought to be built on old Pagan sites of worship such as St Michael's Tower on Glastonbury Tor, and St Paul's Cathedral (originally the site of a temple dedicated to Diana). Also, any specific and local area such as a woodland glade or grove which are special to an individual or group.

sacrifice The only sacrifice performed in Paganism is the sacrifice of oneself to greater growth and understanding of the workings of the cosmos and/or deity, the notion of the Great Work, and the understanding of sacrifice as the transformation of force into form.

salamander Fire elemental, usually depicted in the form of small brightly-coloured lizards.

Salem, USA   Town in Massachusetts where witch trials were held in 1692 after a group of children experimented with divination and then began to exhibit symptoms such as convulsions. The local minister and father of one of the children, Samuel Parris, deemed the behaviour to be the result of diabolical possession, and one of the girls charged three women with bewitching them. Hysteria spread, and other women were accused. Those who freely confessed were spared, but nineteen of those who denied the charges brought against them were hanged between 10th June and 22nd September 1692. This irrational outbreak caused revulsion against the trials and they were not continued. Now home to one of America's most public witches, Laurie Cabot, witchcraft is very visible in Salem, somewhat paradoxical since the women hanged were not witches, and yet Cabot continues to claim that she is carrying on the tradition of witches in the area.

salt   Symbol of purity, said to repel witches and demons, now used in Wiccan circles as a means of purifying water, the mixture of salt and water then being used to purify the participants and to asperge the sacred space.

Samhain   See *Hallowe'en*.

Sanders, Alex   (1926–1988) Born Orrell Alexander Carter in Birkenhead to unmarried parents, and one of thirteen children. The family moved to Manchester where his father adopted the surname Sanders, with which Alex grew up and which he took as his legal name by deed pole in 1970. He had two children, Paul and Janice, with his wife Doreen, to whom he was married from 1947 to 1953. Sanders worked for the John Rylands library, where he read classical texts on ritual magic, and was also influenced in childhood by his Welsh maternal grandmother, who hailed from Caernarvonshire and was skilled in folk magic. In addition, his mother took all her sons along to a Spiritualist church where they all became mediums. Sanders acquired a certain degree of fame working as a medium under the pseudonym Paul Dallas in the 1950s; in trance, he could hold in his hands burning coal.

In 1961, he allegedly wrote to local Wiccans whom he had seen on television, but they took a dislike to him and it was apparently not until 1963 that he was initiated into Wicca by a priestess in Derbyshire. However, the year before he lost his job at the library as a result of extolling the virtues of Wicca to the Manchester press. Sanders went on to act as High Priest to a coven in Nottinghamshire, but the group dissolved in 1964 and he then met the seventeen year old Arline Maxine Morris.

They began running a coven together in 1965, were discovered by a local newspaper, and went on to manipulate the media to such an extent that they became the most famous witches in the world by 1966. Such media attention brought many interested people and led to a whole network of covens springing up around them, despite the fact that longer-established Wiccans denounced Alex as a charlatan. He responded by claiming that his grandmother had initiated him at the age of seven, and allowed his followers to give him the title King of the Witches.

By the close of the 1960s, Alex Sanders had established his own version of the Craft, which became known as Alexandrian Wicca. His claim to have been initiated into the Craft after finding his grandmother, Mary Bibby, celebrating a ritual nude in the kitchen was largely disbelieved, for Alexandrian Wicca is quite clearly based along Gardnerian lines, with greater emphasis on ritual ceremonial magic, angels and spirits, and magical healing. It is claimed by some witches that Sanders created his own tradition because he was refused initiation into Gardnerian covens, but that he managed to obtain a copy of the Gardnerian Book of Shadows which he used as the basis for his tradition.

In 1967, he and Maxine moved to London, and were married on May Day 1968. Of their two children, Maya was born in 1967 and Victor in 1972. In 1969, Sanders was sensationally publicised in a newspaper article which led to many media appearances, a romanticized biography, *King of the Witches*, by June Johns (1969), and a film 'Legend of the Witches' (1969). They continued to run a coven, training and initiating many new members, and as Sander's fame reached its peak Alexandrian Wicca grew exponentially. In 1973, the relationship between Alex and Maxine broke down and they divorced in 1982 but remained friends. Despite frequently proposing remarriage to Maxine, Sanders married Jill in 1986 but the relationship lasted less than a year. Whilst Maxine continued to run the coven, Alex retired somewhat from the limelight to Bexhill and then St Leonards, Sussex, where he continued to teach Wicca, and initiated people from continental Europe. He died of lung cancer in hospital in Hastings on Beltane Eve, 1988 and his pagan funeral took place at Hasting's crematorium on 11th May. His death certificate gave his occupation as 'occultist'.

Sanders, Maxine (b. 1946) Daughter of Victor and Doris Morris, Arline Maxine Morris was given a strict Catholic upbringing in Manchester, including a convent education, and was disowned by her family after the exposure of her activities with Alex and the coven at Alderley Edge by the Manchester paper the *Comet*, which photographed her naked on the altar stone, unbeknown to her. A psychic as a child, she found witchcraft welcomed her gifts instead of frowning on them.

Satanism   A phenomenon distinctly separate from Wicca and Paganism, in that belief in Satan requires a Christian cosmology. Some Satanists worship Lucifer, but for the most part no particular deity is venerated and Satanism can perhaps best be characterised as a creed based on hedonistic occultism. Perhaps the most prominent Satanist is Anton Szandor la Vey founder, in 1966, of the Church of Satan in California.

scarlet woman   A reference to the Book of Revelation which closes the New Testament, Aleister Crowley's priestesses, used in sexual magic, were referred to as scarlet women in keeping with his predisposition to call himself the Great Beast.

Score, John   (1914–1979) Pagan revivalist who founded and edited *The Wiccan* inter-coven newsletter in 1968 which actively promoted the re-emergence of Paganism and led to the foundation of the Pagan Front in 1970.

scourge   The most controversial of the working tools of Wicca, the scourge is a symbol of power and domination, purification and enlightenment but it also has a physical purpose in that light strokes can be used to stimulate the blood and direct it away from the brain, thus causing an altered state of consciousness. It was introduced by Gerald Gardner, who had a particular interest in flagellation, and in some Gardnerian covens all members are scourged before each ritual as a means of purification. Many other covens use the scourge physically only during initiations, and the tails of the scourge are often made of ribbons or cotton, thus stressing the symbolic nature of the scourging rather than hinting at any desire to cause physical pain. It thus acts as a reminder of the self-discipline, stability, control and responsibility that is expected of the Wiccan initiate. These qualities also act as reminders that purification and the journey towards enlightenment take place on an inner level, and as the weapon specifically associated with the second degree initiation, it is deemed important in symbolising the passing of power and responsibility to the new High Priest/Priestess for they can no longer rely on their initiators to take responsibility for them.

scrying   Method of divination in which the scryer enters trance and stares into a reflective device, called a speculum, in which pictures telling the future are seen. Speculums are often crystal or glass balls, black mirrors, fishermen's floats, black bowls filled with water, or even natural ponds in moonlight. Sometimes a candle flame is situated behind the scryer or a silver coin is dropped into a bowl of water to provide an added focus for concentration.

Seal of Solomon (hexagram)   Six sided star, called the Seal of Solomon after King Solomon who drew such power from the hexagram etched on his ring that, according to legend, he was able to command demons. Also known as the Star of David in Judaism, the seal increased in popularity in Medieval times, becoming widely used in alchemy and kabbalah, and included in grimoires.

Seax Wica   American derivation of Gardnerian Wicca, devised in 1973 by Ray Buckland, a former Gardnerian High Priest, who became disillusioned with the corruption he perceived to be inherent in the Wiccan structure of the three degrees of initiation, which he felt encouraged egotistical behaviour, and the secrecy which prevented many genuine seekers from becoming witches. The Seax-Wica, or Saxon Wicca tradition, is based on Saxon mythology and has four principle deities – Woden, Frig or Freya, Thunor, and Tiw. It provides for self initiation as well as for initiation by and into a coven, there is only one degree of rank rather than three, and there is no oath of secrecy. In fact, Seax Wica is openly available to anyone through Buckland's book, *The Tree: Complete Book of Saxon Witchcraft* (1974). In many ways, Seax Wica follows the style of feminist witchcraft, with the annual election of a High Priestess and/or High Priest by all coven members, and collective decision making on matters such as wearing robes or worshipping skyclad, or allowing non-initiates to attend circles as guests. Where it differs from feminist witchcraft, however, is in its emphasis on the High Priest and the male deity as equal in importance to the High Priestess and the female deity.

second degree   Wiccan initiation aimed at facilitating an awareness of the darker side of one's consciousness, exploring the hidden depths, and facing the anima/animus in Jungian terms. It is the initiation which makes the initiate a true priest or priestess of Wicca, and they are given the title High Priest/ess. At its core is an oath more binding than that of the first degree, and the willing of the power of the tradition, which is done by placing hands on the head and under the knees whilst the initiand kneels. The initiate is bound but not blindfold, and is required to use the working tools presented in the first degree initiation. Teachings are given, and the

Legend of the Goddess is enacted by the coven, usually somewhat raucously. In some traditions, second degree initiates are permitted to form their own covens and at the very least are expected to take a greater part in training new and newer initiates in the coven. Second degree initiates are empowered to initiate others to first and second degree.

secrecy   Required in Wicca and some magical orders, where oaths of secrecy are administered at initiations. See also *oaths*.

seidkona   Asatrú priestess skilled in divination and prophecy, known historically as a volva, the first of which was the goddess Freya.

seidr   A form of witchcraft once practised widely in northern Europe and described in the Edda, knowledge of which was given by the goddess Freya. A wooden platform was erected on which sat the seidkona or volva in a trance, during which she communicated with the world of the gods and was able to answer questions put to her regarding future harvests, animal fecundity, and fates of individuals.

Sekhmet   ('the powerful') Lion-headed Egyptian war goddess, daughter of Ra and known as the Eye of Ra since she was personified as the scorching, destructive power of the sun. Defender of the divine order, she sat in the uraeus in Ra's brow and spat flames at his enemies. When sent to quell a rebellion of men against Ra she became uncontrollable and had to be tricked into drinking beer mixed with pomegranate juice to slake her thirst for blood.

self-initiation   An arguable concept which still elicits some discussion, particularly within Wicca. Some argue that no one initiated the first witch or Wiccan, so therefore self-initiation must be valid. Others respond that self-initiation is invalid because there is nothing one can initiate oneself into, that the tradition requires transmission from those already in the tradition. They argue that a more appropriate term is self-dedication, which allows for dedication to a particular deity or way of life, but does not lay claim to initiation into an established tradition. Whilst most would agree that anyone can call themselves a witch, Wicca does not accept as Wiccans those who have not been initiated by those already initiated to second or third degree in Wicca.

Servants of the Light   British magical fraternity established in the 1970s which arose as a splinter organisation from the Society of the Inner Light founded by Dion Fortune in 1922.

1734 Tradition North American witchcraft tradition derived from Robert Cochrane's practices which he claimed pre-dated Gardner's Wicca and which he may have called the Order of 1734. Joseph Wilson founded the tradition in the USA after corresponding with Cochrane for the year before the latter's death in 1966. He began teaching the tradition in California in the mid-1970s through two covens, the Gliocas Tuatha and later the Temple of the Elder Gods, from which all present 1734 Tradition covens stem. Later research to trace the roots of 1734 by Ann and Dave Finnin of the Roebuck led them to the conclusion that such a tradition never existed in Britain. It seems more likely that 1734 derived from a misreading of the date 1724 on a plate bought by Doreen Valiente in an antiques shop and given to Cochrane to use in rituals to carry the cakes. Cochrane allowed a photograph of the plate to be included in Justine Glass' book *Witchcraft, the Sixth Sense – and Us* (1965), a book which contained considerable input from Cochrane as well as Doreen Valiente, claiming it as a ritual tool passed down through his family over the centuries. Another claim is that 1734 refers not to a date but to a special numerological value derived from Graves' *The White Goddess*. See also *Cochrane, Robert; Regency.*

sexuality Is affirmed in Paganism, the body is regarded as sacred and sex between consenting adults is celebrated as a sacred rite. See also *Great Rite, Third Degree.*

Seymour, Charles Richard Foster (1880–1943) Irish soldier and occultist who became a member of Dion Fortune's Fraternity of the Inner Light in the 1930s and was initiated into Co-Masonry in 1941. He wrote *The Old Religion – A Study in the Symbolism of the Moon Mysteries* (1968) and was particularly interested in Celtic spirituality. He worked extensively with his priestess, Christine Hartley.

shamanism A technique and practice which is of growing importance in modern Paganism. The term 'shaman' derives from the Tungus people of Siberia, whence shamanism originated before spreading from the Russian steppes westwards into Europe and eastwards into North America; it has also been found in South America and the Pacific. Thus, historically, shamanism can be found throughout the world, and the term has now come to be applied generally to anyone who takes on the role of mediating between the human and spirit worlds. Elements of shamanism are found throughout European Paganism, but are most obvious in Finno-Ugric religion where Vainamoinen the First Shaman, son of Ilmater Water-Mother, the Creatrix Goddess, helps complete the creation of the world. The growth of modern neo-shamanism began with Mircea Eliade's classical study *Shamanism: Archaic Techniques of Ecstasy* (1951), becoming more popular as a form of 'spiritual ecology' in the 1960s; however, it was not until the 1980s that non-academic publications and organisations regarding modern-day shamanism appeared. Shamans of today range from those trained in the path of a particular society, such as a First Nations tribe, to those reconstructing shamanic experience from historical accounts and their own experience.

Traditionally, a shaman is one set apart, usually identified at an early age as possessing special powers of communication with the otherworld: their role is to negotiate and maintain relations between human and spirit communities. Often they have had a spontaneous, severe and traumatic experience – an illness or spiritual crisis – which forced open for them the doors of the otherworld. The work of the shaman is considered dangerous and, in many societies, to be a shaman is seen as much as a curse as a blessing. To the shaman, the spirit world is viewed as part of everyday reality, surrounding us, and the shaman has the ability to move between the worlds and thus provide a bridge, becoming a pathfinder for his people. Shamanism involves techniques of ecstasy, and through training or calling the shaman is able to access the spirit worlds and work with the powers there for healing, divination and magic. Shamans place great emphasis on personal experience, and therefore usually follow a solitary path though some work together in groups.

shapeshifting   Process by which people are believed to be able to change their form into that of an animal, bird or insect, particularly witches who were believed to change into hares, dogs, crows, cats and other creatures. During the Great Witch Hunt, witches were accused of and admitted to shapeshifting, but it is often claimed that such stories were the result of the use of hallucinogenic ointments which led to deep sleep during which the witch dreamed of travelling in the form of an animal. Shapeshifting is also very prevalent in shamanism, where the shaman is believed to have the power to shapeshift into his or her guardian animal spirit through the consumption of hallucinogens or other consciousness-altering techniques such as dancing and drumming. Shapeshifting remains a popular concept in Paganism, particularly in visionary practices such as pathworking.

sigils   Visual stimulus which symbolises a concept or intent used in magical workings. A specific form of magic known as sigil magic is derived from the work of Austin Osman Spare and is widely used in chaos magic.

Sigrblot   Festival marking the beginning of the summer, celebrated by many modern Heathens.

Simos, Miriam   See *Starhawk*.

Sjöö, Monica   Artist and theoretician of the reemerging goddess religion, co-author with Barbara Mor of *The Great Cosmic Mother: Rediscovering the Religion of the Earth* (1987).

skyclad   Euphemism for ritual nudity. The term may have derived from a Jain sect in India, the *digambaras* (meaning 'skyclad') which believed that no clothing should be worn by the true ascetic.

solitary   Practitioner of magic or any Pagan tradition who works predominantly alone or with their partner rather than in a group, grove or coven. See also *Hedgewitchcraft*.

solstices   Two points in the year when the sun is furthest from the equator at noon, marked by the longest and shortest days of the year, the summer and winter solstices respectively, which in the northern hemisphere occur around 21st June and December (for the southern hemisphere, the winter solstice is in June and the summer solstice in December). The solstices are celebrated as two festivals in the Wheel of the Year under a variety of names, including Midsummer/Litha and Midwinter/Yule.

sorcery   Form of witchcraft derived from a concoction of Paganism and Christianity which practices the manipulation of natural forces for a particular purpose and the casting of spells, often categorised as 'low' magic. The term derives from the Latin *sortiarius* ('diviner') and the French *sorcier* ('sorcerer'/'witch').

Sorcerer's Apprentice, The   Large store and mail order for the occult run by Chris Bray in Leeds. He used the Sorcerer's Apprentice to set up a fighting fund for Pagans faced with legal action and worked for public acceptability of Paganism. In 1989, he undertook the Occult Census, which led to the much-quoted estimate that there were 250,000 witches in the UK. His store was firebombed in the early 1990s.

south   Direction associated with the element of fire, with midday, summer, and colours such as orange and red. Its elemental king is Notus, the Greek name for the south wind.

Southern Coven of British Witches   See *New Forest Coven*.

Spare, Austin Osman   (1888–1956) English artist and occultist who produced work whilst in a trance. Spare believed strongly in reincarnation and theorised that the purpose of humankind was to use trance and sigils to trace previous existences to their primal roots. He was a member of Aleister Crowley's Argenteum Astrum for a short time, but developed his own magical system known as Zos which was based on the premise that the human body is the ideal vehicle through which the spiritual and occult forces of the universe become manifest. He claimed to be possessed by William Blake, whose work he tried to emulate.

spear   Associated with the element of fire, the spear is one of the eight weapons of the ancients.

speculum   Device used in scrying, such as magic mirror, crystal ball, or glass floats.

spell   Form of words used as a magical charm or incantation.

spirit   The fifth element, see *Aether*.

spirit of place   Otherwise known as the *genius loci*, the spirit of the place is that which makes itself known as the inhabitant or guardian of a specific locale and can thus be worked with magically to protect that place, as in eco-magic. It is a concept which is used extensively by environmental Pagan groups such as Dragon Environmental Network.

Spiritualism   Religious movement which began in the USA in 1848 in New York when the Fox sisters claimed to have communicated with spirits through a system of rappings. This led to the formation of Spiritualist Churches and societies, where seances were held and mediums attempted to communicate with dead loved ones. Spiritualism was well-established in Britain by 1860, where it provided an alternative to the Christianity which many were becoming disillusioned with as a result of the Darwinian controversy. In this movement, where hell had no place, many found sanctuary from the eternal damnation that popular Victorian theology offered them. Many Christians far preferred the concept of an eternal spirit life in which one could still keep in contact with and aid loved ones on earth to the prospect of entering a state of limbo until, at the Last Judgement, they would be sentenced to either Heaven or Hell. Socially,

Spiritualism was seen as a means of arresting the flood of materialism which many saw as threatening to submerge the Western world.

Many Victorian Spiritualists were free thinkers who rejected mainstream religious practice and belief and combined a subversive socialism with a taste for the occult. The Spiritualist movement openly advocated the feminism that had begun to emerge in the mid-Nineteenth Century, bringing upon itself the anathematization of the Roman Catholic Church – in 1864, Spiritualist writings were put on the Index and the movement was denounced by the Vatican in 1898 and again in 1917.

Sprengel, Anna   (d.1890) The alleged German adept from whom W. W. Westcott received the authority to establish the Isis Urania Temple of the Golden Dawn in 1887.

Spring Equinox   One of the four lesser sabbats of the Wheel of the Year, celebrated when light and dark are equal but as light is about to start growing, c. 21st March in the northern hemisphere (c. 21st September in the southern hemisphere). It is also known as Ostara or Eostre, after the Saxon goddess who gave her name also to the Christian Easter. In nature, spring is really beginning and this festival marks the more recognisable growth – flowers and leaves are appearing, and sowing begins in the fields. The sap is rising and spring energy is in abundance – God and Goddess come together impelled by primeval sexual drive. After their coupling, the Goddess is pregnant, but the God continues his roaming and does not stay with her. The equality of day and night is taken to represent the God's position, equipoised between the unconscious, animal instinct and growing conscious awareness, and the step forward is recognised as a time to experiment with more outgoing activities than the winter hibernation has allowed. Eggs are often painted and used to decorate the Spring Equinox altar, symbolising new life breaking forth.

stang   A ritual tool used in witchcraft which consists of a forked wooden staff, usually of ash, which stands in the northern point of the circle to symbolise either the presence of the Hornèd God or of the Goddess according to how it is placed. The forks are often decorated with foliage and flowers according to the season. The stang is regarded as a symbol of fertility when pushed into the earth, and as a guardian of the circle. It can also represent the world ash tree Yggdrasil, acting as a bridge between the worlds. It is particularly used in Robert Cochrane's form of witchcraft, and may have been derived from the forked staff of the Berber Dhulqarneni cult, described in a book by Idries Shah published in 1962.

Starhawk (Miriam Simos) (b. 1951) One of the most prominent feminist Pagan activists in the United States, Starhawk has actively reclaimed her Jewish roots as well as being a witch, an exploration which has led to her sometimes referring to herself as a 'Jewitch'. Her feminist activism in the 1970s led her to the Goddess movement, and she studied feminist witchcraft with Z. Budapest and Fairy Witchcraft with Victor Anderson. After practising as a solitary, Starhawk formed Compost, her first coven, from participants in an evening class on witchcraft and then a second, Honeysuckle, for women only. She was elected president of the Covenant of the Goddess from 1976–77, published her first book, *The Spiral Dance* in 1979, and was one of the founders of the Reclaiming Collective in San Francisco in 1980.

The Spiral Dance has proved to be an ever-popular volume since it was first published in 1979, selling over 100,000 copies in its first ten years of publication. The book is based on Anderson's Fairy tradition but incorporates strictly feminist principles into modern witchcraft, principles which are expanded in her later books *Truth or Dare* (1987) and *Dreaming the Dark* (1988). Starhawk combines nature worship, politics, activism, psychology, and Goddess worship in an attempt to heal spiritual and political divisions in society and individuals. Such themes come out even more strongly in her two novels, *The Fifth Sacred Thing* (1993) and *Walking to Mercury* (1997). European Wiccan attitudes towards Starhawk's redirection of witchcraft towards political activism tend to be cautious.

Stella Matutina (Order of the Companions of the Rising Light in the Morning) A splinter group of the Golden Dawn, formed after its split in 1903. More mystically-inclined members such as A. E. Waite set up a new temple which followed a path which was vaguely oriented towards Christian mysticism and rejected ritual magic. The more magically inclined, led by R. W. Felkin, formed the Stella Matutina which attempted to restore communication with the secret chiefs of the third order of the Golden Dawn, the mystical Rosicrucian forces, who would provide new spiritual direction. From 1910, Felkin was in close contact with Rudolf Steiner's German Rosicrucian group, under the influence of which Felkin reorganised the Stella Matutina along more theosophical lines. The temple was closed in 1919, just before Felkin emigrated to New Zealand.

Stonehenge Bronze Age monument in Wiltshire, often connected with Druids despite archaeological evidence pointing to the termination of building work there by 1100 BCE and the lack of any evidence suggesting that Druids ever worshipped there subsequently. The use of Stonehenge by modern Druids and other Pagans is based on the seventeenth century romantic connections made by John Aubrey, who associated Druids with Stonehenge in his 1659 work *Monumenta Brittanica*. His theories were discredited but nevertheless were picked up by the Lincolnshire doctor and antiquarian William Stukeley. In 1740, Stukeley published *Stonehenge, a Temple restor'd to the British Druids* in which he perpetuated the myth and expanded it to suggest that both Stonehenge and Avebury had been built by the ancient Celtic priesthood and were therefore Druid temples. This myth has been important in modern Druidry, who still celebrate the Midsummer and Midwinter solstices at the henge when permission is granted by English Heritage.

Summerlands Mythical place regarded by Pagans as a paradise, the Land of Eternal Youth, in which spirits of the dead are rejuvenated, rested, and prepared for rebirth. The term was used in Celtic studies for the Gaelic otherworld, and by Blavatsky, who regarded it as one of the higher astral realms.

Summers, Montague (1880–1948) Christian author and scholar who wrote extensively on the subject of witchcraft and translated sixteenth and seventeenth century manuscripts including the *Malleus Maleficarum*.

Sun An important symbol of the male aspect of the universe and thus of the Hornèd God, who is reborn with the sun at the winter solstice, grows in strength and power until the summer solstice, when he reigns as the sun king before being sacrificed at Lammas and moving on to become king of the underworld. Sun goddesses are, however, also popular.

Susan B. Anthony Coven Women-only coven founded by Zsusanna Budapest in Los Angeles, California in 1971, named after the leader of the women's suffrage movement. By 1976, it had a core of some twenty women, but as many as three-hundred participated in some of its activities and related covens were formed in five other states. When Budapest moved to Oakland in the early 1980s, the coven continued without her for some years before disbanding, at which point Budapest started a coven of the same name in Oakland.

sweatlodges Popular in many forms of Paganism, particularly Druidry, the sweatlodge has been borrowed from the Lakota and other American Indian peoples. The lodges are temporary domed structures made from a framework of wood covered with a tarpaulin. The intent is to exclude all light and make of the lodge a creative womb. Rocks are then heated in a fire outside and brought into the lodge. The people then sit in total darkness around the incandescent rocks, and this produces an intense experience which is used for purification as the body sweats out impurities, rededication to the earth, for sorting out problems, for ritual. Preparation for a sweatlodge includes fasting, building the lodge, collecting wood, and building a spirit trail. Both preparation and time in the lodge are regarded as part of the same ritual and are treated as sacred.

Swedenborg, Emmanuel (1688–1772) Born in Stockholm, Sweden, Swedenborg was a distinguished scientist and held a seat in the House of Nobles of the Swedish parliament before undergoing a profound religious crisis in 1743–44 during which he experienced trances, talking with Jesus, angels, devils and departed human souls – Moses, Saint Paul, Luther, Calvin, popes and kings. He became convinced that the Lord had chosen him to be the Bible's infallible interpreter, and devoted the rest of his life to what he regarded as his divine mission – to teach mankind the true meaning of the scriptures. Swedenborg published many works, including the eight-volume *Arcana Coelestia* (1756), *The Earths in the Universe* (1758), *The New Jerusalem and its Heavenly Doctrine* (1758), *On the Intercourse Between the Soul and the Body* (1769), *Divine Love and Wisdom* (1763), *The Apocalypse Revealed* (1766), and lastly, *The True Christian Religion* (1771). He taught a pantheistic theosophy centred on Jesus Christ, whom he felt embodied a Trinity of Love, Wisdom and Energy. He regarded the human body as the kingdom of the soul, and this led him to develop his doctrine of correspondence – that all phenomena of the physical world have their spiritual correspondences. Swedenborg did not believe in Christian redemption and believed that there was no such thing as a personal Devil or Satan. After his death in London at the age of 85, the Church of the New Jerusalem, based on his writings, emerged; the first Swedenborgian congregation in England was founded in the late 1780s, and in the same decade his doctrines were introduced into the United States. Hundreds of psychics and mediums in the nineteenth and early twentieth centuries followed Swedenborg, and his doctrine of correspondence was particularly influential on Western poetic literature, especially the Romantic and Symbolist traditions; he was admired by such people as Baudelaire, Goethe, Blake, and Kant.

sweeping Ritual sweeping with the besom symbolises the sweeping aside of everyday space and time so that attention is focused on ritual; in time, it can in itself be a trigger for entering into an altered state of consciousness. In rituals celebrated outdoors, the sweeping also has the practical purpose of removing objects such as leaves, twigs and small stones from the ritual site, all of which would be painful if trodden on with bare feet.

sword One of the working tools of Wicca, ritual magic, and of many Pagan traditions, the sword is associated with the element of air and is used to cast the circle and at initiations, where the initiate is challenged at the point of a drawn sword.

sylph Air elemental, usually depicted as winged, almost transparent beings, a little like fairies.

T

Taliesin British poet of the sixth century. As Gwion Bach he tended Ceridwen's cauldron and obtained wisdom from the three drops which he sucked from his finger, after which she chased him in various forms before swallowing him when she was a hen and he a grain of corn. He was then reborn from her as Taliesin. See also *awen, cauldron, Ceridwen*.

talisman Magically-empowered object such as a stone or ring believed to confer powers on the bearer, whereas amulets offer protection.

Talking Stick Magical and Pagan moot which meets in London fortnightly for talks and lectures, and produced the single-issue Pagan comic *Wizard and Whips* which took a light-hearted and, indeed, comic look at Paganism and the occult. Talking Stick is now called 'The Secret Chiefs'.

Tara Sacred hill in County Meath, Ireland, once the residence of the High Kings of Ireland. Also the name of a diverse star goddess of North West India, Nepal and Tibet, whose name means 'radiating'.

tarot A pack of seventy-eight cards, of which twenty-two make up the Major Arcana and the remaining fifty-six make up the Minor Arcana. The tarocco cards first appeared in Italy in the middle of the fifteenth century and were used for games before becoming increasingly employed as a means of divination although later claims tried to suggest that the cards originated in either a Hermetic source (de Gebelin, 1781) or from the kabbalah (Eliphas Lévi, nineteenth century). The tarot was an integral part of the Golden Dawn system of magic, and the most well-known pack after the oldest, the Marseille, is perhaps the Rider-Waite tarot, which was developed by the Golden Dawn member A. E. Waite and drawn by Pamela 'Pixie' Coleman Smith. Other packs include Aleister Crowley's Thoth tarot, drawn by Frieda Harris, and in recent years some packs with specifically Pagan themes and images, such as the Matthews' Arthurian tarot, the Tarot of the Old People, and The Witches Tarot, have become very popular.

taufr Talismans made with runic inscriptions in Heathenism.

teen-witch An image of increasing popularity in the late 1990s, deriving largely from the film *The Craft* (1996), which proved especially influential with teenagers, and from books written specifically for teenagers, in particular Silver Ravenwolf's *Teen Witch* (1998).

temple Place or building regarded as the dwelling place of a deity or deities. Pagans recognise as temples buildings, nature, and people. These may include a room or part of a room set aside within someone's house which is used for solitary or group practices, a local grove or sacred site such as a stone circle, the whole of nature, and humankind.

thealogy A term frequently found in feminist writings to denote a theology focused on the feminine divine, i.e. the Goddess.

Thelema ('will') Religious and occult order founded by Aleister Crowley in 1920, inspired by the writings of the medieval French satirist, François Rabelais, whose *Gargantua* (1534) includes the foundation of a commemorative abbey, the abbey of Thélème. Crowley also drew on Nietzschean philosophy of the will to power and the exaltation of the *Übermensch* (superman), believing that human progress was facilitated by discovering one's own true will and making it manifest. See also *Book of the Law*.

Theosophical Society Occult organisation founded by Helena Petrovna Blavatsky and Colonel Henry Steele Olcott in New York in 1875, open to both men and women for research and study, and introduced to England in January 1883. Its published aims were "First – to form the nucleus of an Universal Brotherhood of Humanity, without distinction of race, creed or colour. Second – to promote the study of Aryan and other Eastern literature, religion and sciences and vindicate its importance. Third – to investigate the hidden mysteries of Nature and the Physical powers latent in man", and also to abolish Christianity and replace it with freethinking humanism. Inspiration was drawn from Egyptian occultism and the Western Esoteric Tradition and later from India, the embodiment of Oriental wisdom which, according to Blavatsky, surpassed that of the West. Clearly, the Theosophists did not succeed in overthrowing Christianity, but they did provide a forum for debate and study of many religions and did a great deal to popularise Indian religions in particular, especially under Annie Besant. The Society is still in existence today.

theurgy   Early Neoplatonic system of white magic which involves the invocation of entities such as angels to secure divine or supernatural help in human affairs.

Third Degree   Last of the formal Wiccan degrees of initiation, the third degree centres upon the Great Rite which is performed either symbolically (in token) or in actuality (in true). A third degree initiate is empowered to initiate others to first, second and third degree.

thirteen   A number associated with bad luck and with witchcraft, particularly after Margaret Murray's assertions that all covens consisted of twelve members plus one leader, which meet at the thirteen full moons of the year.

Thor   Norse god of thunder, weather, agriculture and the home, son of Odin and Frigga, usually portrayed armed with a hammer.

Thor's Hammer   (*'mjölnir'*) Symbol used in modern Heathenism to indicate affinity to the Norse god Thor and also as a symbol of Heathenism in general. It represents the endless spinning energy of the universe, the wheel of life, which is wielded to support the evolution of life, inspiring strength. It is regarded as symbolising Heathenism's vitality and energy, reflecting the centrality of energetic nature to the Heathen religion and its strength as a revived tradition.

Three-Fold Law   A Wiccan law which states that whatever you do, whether for good or bad, will return to you threefold. See also *ethics*.

thyrsus   Ivy-twined, pine-cone tipped staff sacred to Dionysus. It is an obvious phallic symbol which was thought to have magical properties which could be used to obscure the identity of the carrier.

tiphareth ('beauty') Sixth and central sephiroth on the kabbalistic tree of life, symbolised by the sun and representing balance.

Tir na' n'og Irish Celtic land of perpetual youth.

Traditional Craft (North America) Term used in the USA and Canada to denote branches of Gardnerian and Alexandrian Wicca which can trace their lineage back to Gardner or Sanders and which retain the original, English practice and understanding of Wicca as opposed to the myriad derivations to be found in the States.

Traditional witchcraft (UK) Form of witchcraft which overlaps with Hereditary witchcraft, as Traditional witches may also be from an Hereditary line. Both claim to predate the Gardnerian revival and were reputedly furious with Gerald Gardner for popularising the old religion, regarding such enterprises as his witchcraft museum on the Isle of Man as a disaster. Traditional groups comprise a number of different and separate localised traditions which have brought in outsiders, some of whom have subsequently transplanted the tradition to other countries. Moon magic, moon lore, rural wisdom and communication with the spirits of the dead are emphasised, and belief in reincarnation, and concepts of deities as personifications of powers of nature or universal life (feminine and masculine, God and Goddess) is common. Witches from both Traditional and Hereditary witchcraft tend to refer to their religion simply as the Craft or witchcraft; Wicca is more commonly reserved for Gardnerians, Alexandrians, and other modern traditions.

trance Semi-conscious state which lowers the reaction to external stimuli and allows the trance state person to focus on the inner realm of the imagination.

transcendence The idea of a god or gods existing apart from the material world is contrary to Paganism, which follows a philosophy of immanence rather than transcendence.

Tree of Life A common glyph found in many religions, often showing the emanations of the divine, the relationship between humans and the divine, interacting worlds etc. The tree of life is symbolic of the entire universe and its patterns of interaction; examples include Yggdrasil and the kabbalistic Tree of Life.

Tree Calendar   Calendar derived by Robert Graves from the Gaelic alphabet of thirteen consonants and five vowels, in which the eighteen letters of the alphabet are mythologically associated with certain trees. January 21st, for example, is the first day of the Rowan, February 18th the first day of the Ash, July 8th the first day of the Holly, and December 23rd day of the Yew and Silver Fir. It has become popular in some Pagan traditions, particularly Druidry.

trees   Often associated with magical lore, regarded as the haunts of witches and fairies, and used as sites of worship by Celts and Druids. The rowan, for instance, was regarded as a protector against witches, whilst the elder and thorn are witches' trees. The association of trees with life, fertility and wisdom has led to their use to symbolise the universe, with their branches the heavens, trunks the earth, and roots the underworld. Thus, in Scandinavian mythology Yggdrasil represents the World Tree, or Tree of Life. An oak tree was adopted as the symbol of the Pagan Federation in the 1990s, and the protection and planting of trees is popular among Pagans.

Triple-Goddess   Ancient goddess form in Græco-Roman religion and in Celtic images of fertility. Examples include the three Graces, the three Fates, the three Furies, the triple Moon Goddess Artemis/Selene/Hecate, and the nine (3x3) Muses. The idea of a triple goddess was promulgated by Jane Ellen Harrison in *Prologomena to the Study of Greek Religion* (1903), and thence became a central motif of witchcraft and Wicca, where the triple goddess is associated with the moon and envisaged as maiden/waxing moon, mother/full moon, and crone/waning moon. The dark moon period is associated with the fourth face of the goddess which cannot be seen. Such imagery is important in that it reflects the life of women through virgin, mother and crone, as well as birth, sexuality, wise woman, and death, and these in turn lend themselves to a reflection of the seasonal changes.

U

Underworld   The land ruled by the Hornèd God as Lord of Death in Wicca, which draws on the Mesopotamian legend of Innana's descent to the underworld to challenge the forces of darkness embodied in

Ereshkigal, and on the *Brisinga men* story where the Norse goddess Freya journeys to the underworld and obtains the golden necklace fashioned by the dwarves. The goddess descends in search of the answer to death, asking why all things she loves must die, and having got her answer, the Lord of Death presents her with a necklace, to symbolise life. See also *Legend of the Goddess; necklace.*

Universal Declaration of Human Rights   The link, even if only mythical, between Wicca, Paganism and the persecution of women during the Great Witch Hunt, has made Article 18 of the declaration of human rights fundamentally important to Paganism. It reads: everyone has the right to freedom of thought, conscience and religion; this right includes freedom to change his religion or belief, and freedom, either alone or in community with others and in public or private, to manifest his religion or belief in teaching, practice, worship and observance.

US Wicca   Wicca as it was traditionally practised in Britain was exported to the United States by Raymond Buckland in the 1960s where it was transformed into a very different kind of religion, adopting a less formal and hierarchical ritual style, embracing Native American influences such as shamanism and drumming, melding psychotherapy with Wicca, and moving into the realms of political activism. In particular, Wicca was adapted by the women's spirituality movement, resulting in the development of Pagan Goddess spirituality and feminist witchcraft traditions such as Dianic and Reclaiming witchcraft. There are now numerous derivations, some calling themselves Wicca, others using witchcraft.

undine   Water elemental, often depicted as female, regarded as mischievous and treacherous. The word was invented by Paracelsus from the Latin *unda*, 'wave'.

V

Valiente, Doreen   (1922–1999) One of the key figures in modern Wicca and a well-repected witch. She worked with Gerald Gardner as his High Priestess and revised his Book of Shadows, before falling out with him over ever-increasing publicity seeking and leaving his coven in 1957. She was initiated into Robert Cochrane's Clan of Tubal Cain coven in 1964, but left in 1966 having become disillusioned by his fabrications and annoyed by his attacks on Gardnerian witches through the *Pentagram*, journal of the Witchcraft Research Association of which she was president in 1964. Valiente periodically withdrew from the public face of Wicca, but was consistent in her support for the old Pagan religions. In 1971, she was a founder member of the Pagan Front, and in November 1998 she spoke at the annual Pagan Federation conference in London. Her life within Wicca, witchcraft and Paganism is documented in her books *The Rebirth of Witchcraft* (1989), *Witchcraft for Tomorrow* (1978), and *Witchcraft: A Tradition Renewed* (1990, with Evan Jones).

Valkyries ('chooser of the slain') In Norse mythology Odin's twelve handmaidens, who hovered over battlefields and carried to Valhalla the slain warriors chosen by the Gods.

Vanatrú ('trust in the Vanir') Name used by some Heathens to denote their affinity with the Vanir gods rather than the Aesir gods.

Vanir Germanic and Norse deities concerned with the peace and fertility of the earth, in conflict with the Aesir sky gods. They include Njord, Frey and Freya, and are important in Asatrú and Heathenism.

visualisation Making something visual in one's mind, especially something not visible to the eye, e.g. the circle which is cast at the beginning of a ritual, the Lords of the Elements etc. Visualisation exercises form an important part of Wiccan training, and in Paganism generally the imagination is regarded as an active power which both perceives and creates realities, operating as the magical intermediary between thought and being. Imagination is not the same as fantasy, but since imagination as a creative function is incompatible with a worldview which denies the existence of an intermediate universe between the universe of empirical, sensory data and a meta-empirical, spiritual universe, it has been degraded into fantasy. In visualisation, the imagination is trained to perceive different realities, to give form to that which is beyond form. Thus, in imagining a flaming red pentagram, Pagans not only see into the realm of fire, but are enabled to move into that very reality itself.

volva Priestess concerned with divination and prophecy in ancient Norse religion, also known as seidkona. The term derived from the word 'volr', a cyclindrical object, which in turn comes from a root meaning 'to turn'.

Waite, Arthur Edward (d.1942) Influential occultist and Christian mystic, a Freemason and member of the Societas Rosicruciana in Anglia, and member of the Golden Dawn from 1890 to 1903 when he left to form part of the triumvirate heading the reconstituted Second Order which retained the name of the Isis Urania Temple and the Golden Dawn rituals. The latter were reworked in 1910. Always uncomfortable with magic, Waite founded the Fellowship of the Rosy Cross in 1915, including an inner order of Masons and Theosophists called the Ordo Sanctissimus Roseae et Aureae, which survived until his death in 1942.

walknot A symbol of the Norse god Odin formed from three interlocked triangles, often worn by Heathens to denote their affinity to him.

wand One of the eight working tools of Wicca, long associated with magic. Often made of hazel, it symbolises the will and is associated with the element of fire (or the element of air, according to some traditions). Wands can be simple pieces of wood cut from a tree, or more elaborate with tips made from pine cones, crystals, or amber, or with painted stems. Magical energy is directed through the wand and out through the tip.

waning moon Period of time in which the moon passes from full to dark, associated with the crone or hag aspect of the goddess, and with magic to wind something down (e.g. reduce tumours).

warlock A term popularly used for a male witch, derived from the Old English *waer* (truth) and *logan* (to lie), i.e. an oathbreaker.

Warriors of Pan Pagan organisation founded in the 1930s in England. Similar to the scouting movement, it was open to adults and children, who became either warriors or handmaidens, and taught woodcraft Paganism at summer camps.

watchtowers   A term borrowed from the Enochian magic of Dr John Dee, used for the Elemental Lords. See *Elemental Lords*.

water   One of the four mundane elements, associated with the westerly direction and the west wind Zephyrus, colours such as green, blue and turquoise, death and initiation, reflection, emotions, the Moon, and zodiac signs Cancer, Scorpio and Pisces.

waxing moon   Period of time in which the moon passes from new to full, associated with the maiden aspect of the goddess, considered a powerful time of growth.

Weatherwax, Esmerelda (Granny)   The village witch of Bad Ass in the kingdom of Lancre in Terry Pratchett's Discworld series, but as she considers herself to be the greatest witch on the Discworld, she sets no limits to her domain.

west   Direction associated with the element of water, with evening, autumn, and colours such as blues and greens. Its elemental king is Zephyrus, the Greek name for the west wind.

Westcott, William Wynn   (b.1848) Coroner, Freemason and General Secretary (1882) and Supreme Magus (1892) of the Societas Rosicruciana in Anglia. Westcott was an expert on the kabbalah and Hermetism, and was prominent in Anna Kingsford's Hermetic Society. He was one of the founders of the Hermetic Order of the Golden Dawn, from which he retired in 1897 once his position there became known to the authorities, probably as a result of Mathers' desire to rid himself of rivals to the leadership of the Order. See also *Hermetic Order of the Golden Dawn*.

Western Esoteric Tradition   A vast field comprising a body of material gathered together in the West since the end of the fifteenth century, including the kabbalah, hermeticism, Gnosticism, neo-Pythagoreanism, and Stoicism and the occult sciences of astrology, alchemy, and magic. All these components are considered to be mutually complementary, and to have emerged via representatives of the *philosophia perennis* such as Moses, Zoroaster, Hermes Trismegistus, Plato, Orpheus, and the Sibyls. The main focus of the Western Esoteric Tradition is the connections between the individual and the universe, the universal and the particular, microcosm and macrocosm, exemplified in six currents: correspondences, living nature, imagination and mediation, experience of transmutation, the praxis of the concordance, and transmission. Since its inception in the Renaissance, the Western Esoteric Tradition has acted as a force against a mechanistic worldview, offering instead an organic worldview, and a science based on religious attitudes rather than one based wholly on secular principles. In a very real sense, it created the conditions necessary for the emergence of contemporary Paganism and its forerunners, and continues to exert considerable influence.

Western Mysteries   Name given to occult and magical groups descended from Dion Fortune's Fraternity of the Inner Light, including its direct descendant, the Society of the Inner Light. Western Mysteries groups tend to follow the western mystery traditions of Eleusis and Egypt, Druidry, Kabbalah, and elements of Mithraism, and are run by adepts. Three degrees of initiation are common, as is a belief in reincarnation and spiritual progression.

Wheel of the Year   The name given to the cycle of eight seasonal festivals found in Wicca and Druidry, now celebrated with rituals by the majority of Pagans. The festivals consist of two groups: the fire festivals, cross-quarter days, or Greater Sabbats of Candlemas/Imbolc (February 2nd), Beltane (April 30th), Lughnasadh/Lammas (July 31st), and Hallowe'en/Samhain (October 31st), based on the agricultural year, and the solar festivals, or Lesser Sabbats of the Winter and Summer Solstices (c. December 21st and c. June 21st) and the Spring and Autumn equinoxes (c. March 21st and c. September 21st). These are the traditional dates for each festival, but they are not fixed; many groups often find it easier, for the practical purpose of getting everyone together, to work to a set date (usually the nearest Friday or Saturday to the dates given), whilst smaller groups or individuals working alone may choose to wait for a specific sign of nature (e.g. first snowdrop for Imbolc) and celebrate on that day.

The existence of such a calendar is contested, for there is no irrefutable evidence for it and it is unlikely that identical seasonal ceremonies would have been kept throughout the whole of the British Isles, given the variant temperatures, agricultural practices, and daylight hours which exist between the far north of Scotland and the south-western tip of Cornwall. The calendar is most likely an academic construction dating from the eighteenth and nineteenth centuries, but nevertheless the Wheel of the

Year is now of profound importance to an understanding of Paganism, representing the ritual framework of the year in which the seasonal changes in nature are celebrated and symbolised in the myths of Pagan deities. Since the sequence of rituals is cyclical, there is no official beginning. For some, the festival of Samhain or Hallowe'en (October 31st) marks the start of the year, as it is believed to be the ancient Celtic New Year. For others, however, Imbolc (1st February) is the new year, marking the beginning of new growth in early spring.

All groups work rituals differently, though maintaining a common and recognisable framework for both the mythic cycle as a whole and for the particular rituals which are the Wheel of the Year's constituent parts. Thus, each group will celebrate in some way the rebirth of the Sun at Yule, on or near 21st December; the precise content of the ritual, however, varies considerably from year to year and from person to person, and group to group. The style and content of the rituals thus reflect the diversity of Paganism, and not all celebrate all eight festivals: many Heathens, for example, disregard the Wheel of the Year as too recent in origin, preferring to celebrate the festivals of Anglo-Saxon, Teutonic and other Northern European peoples, such as Winternights, Yule, and *Sigrblot*. In whatever format they are celebrated, however, the seasonal festivals of the Wheel of the Year tie in to the ever-changing cycle of Nature and provide a meaningful perspective for this passing of time and by attuning themselves through ritual with the cycles of Nature, Pagans claim to gain greater understanding of their own life cycles.

White Goddess See *Graves, Robert*.

Wicca A religion and mystery tradition which incorporates witchcraft, natural magic, and ceremonial magic into a religious system in which all initiates are members of a priesthood. Organised in small, often intense groups called covens, Wicca does not seek converts but believes that those who are right for their religion, which includes the practice of magic in its rites, holds nature to be sacred, and venerates deity in the form of both gods and goddesses, will find their way to an appropriate coven. Wicca is pragmatic and world embracing, holding that life, the body, and the earth are sacred rather than seeking a way of salvation or escape from earthly existence.

Wicca emerged in 1950s Britain as a highly ritualistic, nature venerating, polytheistic, magical and religious system, which made use of Eastern techniques but operated within a predominantly western framework. It arose from the cultural impulses of the *fin de siècle*, in

153

particular from the occult revival of the 1880s onwards. Various threads were gradually gathered together and woven into Wicca in the 1940s by Gerald Gardner. By the mid-1950s, Wicca had become relatively popular due to Gardner's love of publicity which drew the religion to the attention of the public, and in the early 1960s it was exported to North America. Gardner died in 1964, but his tradition of Gardnerian Wicca was firmly established, much to the annoyance of those who practised Traditional and Hereditary witchcraft, which they believed to be a witchcraft religion older than Gardner's Wicca. Into this stream was injected another current in the 1960s, as Alex Sanders brought a stronger application of high ritual magic to his branch of Wicca. Outside the UK other traditions have evolved, based on Wicca and drawing in their own local or national folklore and culture. In Finland, traditional Paganism has merged with Wicca to form its own unique style of witchcraft, whilst the USA has developed a multitude of derivations, including Faery Wicca, Dianic Wicca and Seax Wicca which have crossed back to Europe.

Wicca can, however, be used to describe very different paradigms. On the one hand, Wicca is used to refer to 'covens' of friends who have no initiation or training but gather together to celebrate the seasons or full moons, a practice which initiatory Wiccans regard as witchcraft or non-aligned Paganism. On the other hand, Wicca is styled as an esoteric religion and mystery tradition operating in small, closed groups to which entry is solely by initiation ceremonies which include oaths of secrecy and which are designed to trigger personal transformation. A shared terminology and understanding of what is and is not 'Wicca' helps maintain important boundaries, aiding the differentiation between Wiccan priests and priestesses who are initiates of the self-styled esoteric mystery religion of Wicca on the one hand, and other forms of witchcraft and Paganism on the other.

The etymology of 'Wicca' is debatable. It has been argued that the word derives from the same root as the Anglo-Saxon word for knowledge, *wit, wittich*, which stems from *weet* meaning 'to know', and such a definition lends itself to modern witches' understanding of themselves as 'wise' men and women who practice the 'Craft of the Wise'. Similarly, some suggest that 'Wicca' derives from *wik*, meaning to 'bend or shape', which links nicely with modern witches' definition of magic, which is to bend or shape energy through will in order to make manifest something on the physical plane. Wicca in fact derives from 'weik' and 'wicce', the Anglo-Saxon word for a *male* witch (female, 'wicce'), the plural form of which may have been 'Wiccan'.

Wiccan, The   Magazine founded by John Score in 1968, which became the magazine of the Pagan Front and then the Pagan Federation. It was published quarterly at the time of the fire festivals, and in 1994 was renamed *Pagan Dawn*. See also *Pagan Front; Pagan Federation*.

Wiccan Church of Canada   Founded in Toronto by Richard and Tamara James, the organisation purchased a collection of Gerald Gardner's letters from Ripley International in 1987. See also *Wilson, Monique*.

Wiccan Rede   A law derived from Aleister Crowley, who in turn adapted it from Rabelais and Neitzsche, to which many witches adhere. "An it harm none, do what thou wilt" is also one of the three principles of the Pagan Federation, and is therefore also known as 'the Pagan Ethic'.

wiccaning   Naming ceremony, the dedication of a baby or child to the deities, the universe, the elements, a celebration of its arrival. Unlike a Christening, no promises are made about the child's future religion.

Wiccecraeft   The original Old English word from which witchcraft is derived, now a modern-day tradition with members drawn from Wicca and Heathenism. It mixes early indigenous plant worship, Anglo-Saxon sorcery and Norse worship of the Vanir, and groups venerate a Lord and Lady (typically Frey and Freya), perform circular dances, and use herbs and trancework in their magic.

widdershins   The anti-clockwise direction, which goes against the sun, and therefore has often been regarded as the direction for 'black' or 'left hand path' magic. In fact, since magic is deemed to be neither good nor bad in Paganism, the direction of movement will depend on the type of magic being worked. Thus, a slow dance to shrink a tumour may be thought more effective if it takes the widdershins direction. It's opposite, clockwise direction is deosil.

Wild Hunt   Nocturnal phantom procession led by Herne the Hunter, particularly associated with Windsor Great Park. See also *Herne*.

will   See *Thelema*.

Williamson, Cecil   (1909–1999) Founder of the Museum of Magic and Witchcraft at Castletown, Isle of Man in 1951 (later sold to Gerald Gardner) and the Witches' House Museum at Boscastle, Cornwall. Along with

Gardner, Williamson did much to publicise Wicca, alongside his museum, in the 1950s and set himself up as a consultant on witchcraft and magic. He claimed to have known witches since early childhood, and to have acted as an M16 agent during World War II. As an agent, he claimed to have helped organise 'Operation Mistletoe', a magical ritual worked by Aleister Crowley against Hitler in Ashdown Forest, Sussex at the behest of M15. The result was the mission of Rudolph Hess to Britain and his capture in 1941. A similar story was told of Gardner's coven in the New Forest, who worked a witchcraft ritual called 'Operation Cone of Power' after France fell in 1940. The purpose of the ritual was to repel Hitler by directing a cone of power against him. After repeating this four times, the strain apparently proved fatal to some of the older members of the coven. It is not clear whether either of these stories contain any truth, but research by Ronald Hutton suggests that the Ashdown Forest 'Operation Mistletoe' is derived from the New Forest 'Operation Cone of Power'. Williamson's Museum is still in business in Boscastle, having been sold to Graham King before Williamson's death.

Wilson, Monique   A high priestess of Gerald Gardner who inherited his museum on the Isle of Man when he died in 1964. In the 1970s, she sold the collection to Ripley's International, a Canadian organization, and it is now housed in Toronto apart from Gardner's letters, which were bought from Ripleys by the Wiccan Church of Canada in 1987. See also *Wiccan Church of Canada*.

Winternights   Anglo-Saxon festival celebrated by many modern Heathens which marks the beginning of winter.

Winter Solstice   See *Yule*.

Witan Assembly   Name of the Odinshof Council, after the Anglo-Saxon royal courts.

WITCH   Acronym of the feminist political protest organisation, the Women's International Terrorist Conspiracy from Hell, formed in 1968, which drew on images of the witch and gypsy as the original guerrilla freedom fighters against oppression. Many feminists, however, found the association with witchcraft unwelcome.

Witch, image of   Western Europe inherited a series of witch images from the *femme fatales* of Classical myth and literature, such as Medea and Circe, and from the hags of Teutonic mythology. The witches depicted in

Shakespeare's *Macbeth* (performed c.1606; published 1623) portray both the hags and the classical tradition through their invocation to Hecate. The image of the witch is ambiguous and complex, holding many connotations in the public mind, most of which are negative. It draws the popular imagination to story-book notions of the 'wicked witch', to the historical persecutions of witches for being 'in league with the devil', and to modern reports of satanic abuse in the sensationalist tabloid press. Somewhat paradoxically, it also tends to hold within it opposing images. Thus, the witch is both an ugly old woman or hag, and a fascinating girl or woman. The witch polarises opinion in the popular imagination: young *and* old, beautiful *and* ugly, the witch is perhaps never quite as she seems; she appears to everyone in a different guise, and we read her according to our own context and expectations. The stereotypical imagery of witchcraft is all saved for the wicked witch, who wears the traditional black robes and pointed hat, has a hooked nose and long finger nails, rides on a broomstick, has strange familiars, and steals children away. This stereotype can be found in cartoons, and in literature, from Shakespeare's three 'secret, black and midnight hags' in *Macbeth* to children's stories, in fairy tales and in film. It even appears on greetings cards and in advertising.

witchcraft   A practice which has a genuinely long trajectory back in time. Initially constituting an old pre-Christian peasant belief that certain people had special powers which could be used to perform beneficial or maleficent magic, those who performed beneficial magic – finding lost goods, healing etc. – were known as 'cunning men' or 'wise women', whilst those who were thought to perform maleficent magic were known as witches. Witchcraft was thus related to magic, and had nothing to do with religion until the sixteenth century when the theological notion that the essence of witchcraft was adherence to the Devil became popular. These two understandings of witchcraft – one old, the other newly introduced from continental Europe – became fused into a new myth in which witches were classed as heretics and could therefore be tried and executed. Still, however, witchcraft was not understood as a religion, but as a particular employment of magic, according to the old belief, using power provided to the witch by the Devil, according to the new theology.

Witchcraft may be perceived as historical use of spellcraft and natural magic on behalf of clients, witchcraft as a craft used to make a living, rather than as a religion, lending itself primarily to images of witches gathered for a sabbat or under a full moon to perform magic and fertility spells. Wicca, on the other hand, tends to define a form of witchcraft which is considered to be more specifically a religion.

Witchcraft Acts   Witchcraft acts in England and Scotland were repealed in 1736, to be replaced with a law which allowed a person to be prosecuted if they were alleged to have magical powers but at the same time denied the possibility that such powers existed. This law was replaced in 1951 by the Fraudulent Mediums Act, which gave freedom for individuals to practice witchcraft so long as no harm was done to person or property. The repeal of the act was brought about by Spiritualists and their supporters rather than by witches: the Labour MP for Barrow-in-Furness, Mr Monslow, argued for religious freedom on behalf of the spiritualists and the Labour MP for Normanton, Mr T. Brooks, argued that the replacement of the 1736 Witchcraft Act with the Fraudulent Mediums Act would remove the grievance and indignity suffered by spiritualists for many years. The bill went through on a nod in June 1951, just a few months before the general election of October that year swept aside Attlee's Labour government. It was, then, hardly a momentous occasion, warranting only a small report in *The Times* of April 1951, and inclusion in a list of assents in *The Times* of June 1951. But to Gerald Gardner, the repeal signified that the time was ripe for the regeneration of Wicca and he set about writing his *Witchcraft Today*, subsequently published in 1954. To those who had read Gardner's earlier works, particularly *High Magic's Aid* (1949), and to those who were inspired by *Witchcraft Today* and *The Meaning of Witchcraft* (1957) to establish covens and initiate witches, the 1951 Repeal was of utmost importance: it offered a chance of religious freedom. In 2001, the year of the fiftieth anniversary of the Repeal, the Pagan Federation appealed to its readership to prepare events to celebrate and remember the repeal of the Witchcraft Act. Pagans in East Anglia compiled a register of those persecuted for witchcraft in that area, and in Lancashire the Lancashire Witch Project was established by those interested in the history of the witch trials, as a means of remembering this anniversary.

Witchcraft Research Association   Organisation founded in February 1964 by Sybil Leek, to provide a forum in which Wiccans could settle their differences and reclaim their own history. She was forced to resign as president by July of that year because she had been popularly linked with acts of ritualised vandalism in Sussex. Leek emigrated to the United States, where she spent the rest of her life, and Doreen Valiente was installed as her successor in August 1964. John Math, a friend of Robert Cochrane, edited the Association's quarterly journal *Pentagram*. The association was short-lived, effectively closing by the end of 1965 due to continued infighting.

Witchcraft Research Centre   Founded and run by Cecil Williamson from the Witches' House Museum, dealing with west country, solitary witchcraft.

Witch Craze   See *Great Witch Hunt*.

Witches' House Museum   Witchcraft museum founded by Cecil Williamson in Boscastle, Cornwall, formerly established at Bourton-on-the-Water, Gloucestershire as the Museum of Witchcraft, the name under which the Boscastle museum now trades.

witches' ladder   Form of spell in which knots are tied into a length of cord whilst a rhyme is chanted.

Witches' Mill   Location of The Folklore Centre of Superstition and Witchcraft, founded by Cecil Williamson in 1951 in the barns attached to a fire-destroyed windmill at Castletown, Isle of Man. The opening ceremony was performed by Gerald Gardner, who subsequently bought the museum from Williamson. It was inherited by Monique Wilson, who sold the contents to Ripley's International, Toronto.

Witches' Rune   In Wiccan ritual, casting the circle is often followed by the raising of power through a circular dance and the chanting of the Witches' Rune, written by Doreen Valiente. In the rune, the formalised gesture used to communicate the stages of removal from the everyday to the magical space gives way to movement controlled only by the rhythm of the chant and the holding of hands in a circle. From the slow circumnambulations which constitute the building up of the circle, the Wiccans join together in a faster, smaller circular movement, in which they feel the power produced by their dancing creating what the Wiccans call the 'cone of power' in the centre of the circle. The chant begins slowly and increases in speed until reaching a crescendo at which point the power is released to fill the circle. It begins:
>Darksome night and shining moon
>East then south then west then north
>Harken to the witches' rune
>Here we come to call thee forth.

wizard   Term derived from the Middle English *wis* ('wise') and used to denote cunning men and white witches in the fifteenth century, and for magicians in the sixteenth and seventeenth centuries. Like warlock, wizard is often popularly used to denote a male witch.

Woden   See *Odin*.

women's mysteries   Vaguely Pagan rituals performed by feminist women who do not regard themselves as witches or Wiccan although they often contain elements of writings by feminist witches such as Starhawk and Z. Budapest. Emphasis tends to be on the earth and moon, life and death, menarche/menstruation/menopause, and the body.

Woodcraft Chivalry, Order of   An organisation founded in New York in 1900 by the Canadian-born Ernest Thompson Seton in an attempt to reform delinquents who were damaging his land. He organised a camp for them, in which they were taught woodcraft, combining 'civilised values' with the practical skills and knowledge of Native American Indians. The impressive results led to the founding of 'tribes' across the United States, and a meeting with Seton in 1906 did much to galvanise Baden-Powell's scout movement in the UK, whose first camp was held in 1907. In 1916 the Order of Woodcraft Chivalry was established in England by Ernest Westlake in the New Forest, Hampshire, and it has been suggested that the Pagan elements of the order, which became more pronounced in the later seceded groups, the Kindred of the Kibbo Kift in 1920 and the schism which created the Woodcraft Folk in 1924, were influential on Gerald Gardner's establishment of Wicca. This suggestion has, however, been proven to be chronologically inaccurate and dubious on the grounds that none of the orders showed any interest whatsoever in witchcraft despite their pagan elements which included sitting round camp fires, chanting, moving deosil around a cast circle, the calling of the four quarters, and the Pan, Artemis, and Dionysus trinity of Woodcraft, with Aphrodite to be honoured at times in recognition of the power of sexuality and alcohol. None of the organisations, however, considered themselves to be Pagan, but were aiming to fuse Christianity and the nature elements of classical paganism in an attempt to reconcile deficiencies in and refresh Christianity, and thus benefit the modern world.

work   Word used to describe ritual or magic among Pagans, derived from its use in Freemasonry: one 'works' a spell or a ritual, rather than 'performs', a term which is perceived as denigrating because it suggests the practitioner is merely acting, or performing theatrics.

working tools   In Wicca, there are eight magical weapons, or working tools, all of which have symbolic meanings. They are presented to the initiate during the first degree initiation ritual. The sword represents the element of air and the trained will, and is also symbolic of an individual group's connection to the greater craft of Wicca; it is traditionally a third degree weapon, and it is necessary to have sword before taking this degree. Usually, one is expected to wait for the right sword to appear and reveal its name. The athame is the personal knife of the witch, and is used for the same purposes as the sword. The white-handled knife is a symbol of aether, and is a binding tool; it is used always within a circle, to cut herbs for incense or inscribe sigils in candles for magical purposes. The wand is a symbol of fire, often made of hazel and sometimes tipped with pine cones, a bead of amber, or other phallic symbol. It represents the will. The pentacle is a weapon of earth and as such has engraved upon it the symbols of Wicca. The censer of incense is a weapon of fire and air, and to some extent of water (from its shape) and earth (due to the resins and herbs burned within it); its smoke provides a link to the divine. The scourge is a second degree weapon, and in many covens second degree initiates are expected to make their own scourge. The cords are symbols of earth, acting as magical conductors down to physical manifestation when used in magic; they are also used in initiations. See also separate entries on each of these tools.

worship   Like 'belief', worship is a problematic term within Paganism. Many Pagans regard it as an inaccurate way of describing their relationship with deity, and prefer to use words such as 'honour', 'revere', 'venerate', or 'work with'.

wyrd Anglo-Saxon term for a concept which defines actions in terms of merit and demerit, similar to the idea of karma or fate. The Norns are the three spinners of the Wyrd, but it is also regarded as a web spun by the actions of many or all beings in which the Norns are central. The web of wyrd is the extension of the wyrd by which an individual moves within the web, the dimensions of, and level of control over which, is dependent on the individual's level of consciousness.

Y

Yeats, William Butler   (1865–1939) Anglo-Irish poet and playwright, leader of the Celtic revival and founder of the Abbey Theatre in Dublin, who was awarded the Nobel Prize for Literature in 1923. A member of the Dublin Hermetic Society from 1885 and the Theosophical Society from 1888, Yeats was initiated into the Golden Dawn in 1890, and introduced Florence Farr to the Order the same year. His magical name of *Festina Lente* was changed in 1893, once he had attained the grade of Adeptus Minor, to a motto of Eliphas Lévi, *Daemon est Deus Inversus*. In 1900, he was made chief of the London Isis Urania Temple, but resigned in 1902 amid troubles regarding the existence of groups within the Order. He joined the Stella Matutina splinter group in 1903, and remained an active member until the 1920s.

Yggdrasil ('horse of Ygg') The World Ash tree which stands at the centre of the nine worlds of gods, giants, dwarves, and men. 'Horse of Ygg' is an epithet of Odin and a euphemism for the gallows tree which recalls the nine nights Odin hung upside down from the tree, pierced by his own spear, in search of occult knowledge. According to Scandinavian and Germanic myth, Yggdrasil is destined to withstand Ragnorak, the day of doom, surviving to provide shelter for those who will repopulate the new earth.

Yule One of the four lesser sabbats of the Wheel of the Year, also known as Midwinter and as the Winter Solstice, and celebrated in the northern hemisphere c. 21st December (c. 21st June in the southern hemisphere). The festival celebrates the birth of the Child of Promise who was conceived at Spring Equinox, representing the rebirth of the son/sun. Symbolically, the festival is seen as a reminder that light dwells in the darkness of the longest night, that life is born in death, from the darkness of the womb which is also understood as the tomb. The Midwinter Solstice marks a transition point between darkness and light, for the longest night is over and daylight will now last longer each day, and Yule thus marks the beginning of the light half of the solar year. In nature, the festival celebrates the fact that the sun will now grow in strength and the life which has been sleeping beneath the surface of the earth will soon begin to sprout forth and clothe the earth. Since the sun is regarded as a symbol of the self, the rebirth of the sun is also taken to represent Pagan's potential for the year ahead, their own rebirth. For this reason, small gifts are often exchanged at Yule rituals during the feasting, in much the same way as they are at Christmas.

Z

zodiac   Astrological configuration of the heavens as a circle divided into twelve segments, each of thirty degrees, as the domains of the constellations of the twelve signs of the zodiac – Aries, Taurus, Gemini, Cancer, Leo, Virgo, Libra, Scorpio, Sagittarius, Capricorn, Aquarius, Pisces. These segments are traversed by the sun over the course of a year, and by the moon and planets over cycles of varying length. Representations of the zodiac date back to ancient times, and are to be found depicted in Egyptian temples such as the temple of Hathor at Dendera.

Select Bibliography

Adler, Margot (1986), *Drawing Down the Moon: Witches, Druids, Goddess-Worshippers, and other Pagans in America Today*, Boston: Beacon Press.

Albanese, Catherine (1990), *Nature Religion in America: From the Algonkian Indians to the New Age*, Chicago: Chicago University Press.

Apuleius, Lucius (1950), *The Transformations of Lucius, otherwise known as The Golden Ass*, trans. Robert Graves, Harmondsworth: Penguin.

Ashcroft-Nowicki, Dolores (1986), *The Ritual Magic Workbook: A Practical Course of Self-Initiation*, London: Aquarian Press.

Aswynn, Freya (1990), *Leaves of Yggdrasil*, St Paul, MN: Llewellyn.

Bachofen, J. J. ([1870], 1967), *Myth, Religion and Mother-Right: Selected Writings* edited by Joseph Campbell, Princeton: Princeton University Press.

Bates, Brian (1983), *The Way of Wyrd*, London: Century.

Bates, Brian (1996), *The Wisdom of the Wyrd*, London: Rider.

Berger, Helen A. (1999), *A Community of Witches: Contemporary Neo-Paganism and Witchcraft in the United States*, Columbia, South Carolina: University of South Carolina Press.

Beth, Rae (1990), *Hedgewitch: A Guide to Solitary Witchcraft*, London: Robert Hale.

Blain, Jenny (2002), *Nine Worlds of Seid-Magic*, London: Routledge.

Bourne, Lois (1998), *Dancing with Witches*, London: Robert Hale.

Bowman, Marion & Graham Harvey (eds), *Pagan Identities,* Special Issue of *DISKUS.* (www.uni-marburg.de/fb03/religionswissenschaft/journal/diskus/).

Briggs, Robin (1996), *Witches and Neighbours: The Social and Cultural Context of European Witchcraft*, London: Harper Collins.

Buckland, Ray (1974), *The Tree: Complete Book of Saxon Witchcraft*, Maine: Samuel Wieser Inc.

Carr-Gomm, Philip (1993), *The Druid Way*, Shaftesbury: Element.

Carr-Gomm, Philip (ed) (1996), *The Druid Renaissance*, London: Thorsons.

Carroll, Peter J. (1987), *Liber Null and Psychonaut*, York Beach, Maine: Samuel Weiser Inc.

Chapman, Malcolm (1992), *The Celts: The Construction of a Myth*, St Martin's Press.

Cohn, Norman (1975), *Europe's Inner Demons*, New York: Basic Books.

Crowley, Aleister (1973), *Magick* ed. John Symonds & Kenneth Grant, Harmondsworth: Arkana.

Crowley, Aleister (1976), *Magick in Theory and Practice*, New York: Dover.

Crowley, Aleister (1983), *The Holy Books of Thelema*, York Beach: Samuel Weiser.

Crowley, Vivianne (1997), *Principles of Wicca,* London: Thorsons.

Crowley, Vivianne (1996), *Wicca: The Old Religion in the New Millennium,* London: Thorsons.

Crowley, Vivianne (1996), *Principles of Paganism,* London: Thorsons.

Crowther, Patricia (1998), *One Witch's World*, London: Robert Hale.

Crowther, Patricia ([1985], 1989), *Lid Off the Cauldron*, Maine: Samuel Weiser Inc.

Daly, M. ([1978], 1981), *Gyn/Ecology: the Metaethics of Radical Feminism*, London: The Women's Press.

Davies, Owen (1999), *Witchcraft, Magic and Culture, 1736–1951*, Manchester: Manchester University Press.

Ehrenreich, Barbara & Deirdre English (1973), *Witches, Midwives and Nurses: A History of Women Healers*, New York: Feminist Press.

Eliade, Mircea (1974), *Shamanism: Archaic Techniques of Ecstasy*, Princeton, NJ: Princeton University Press.

Ellis, Peter B. (1994), *The Druids*, London: Constable.

Faivre, Antoine (1994), *Access to Western Esotericism*, New York: SUNY.

Faivre, Antoine & Needleman, Jacob (eds) (1992), *Modern Esoteric Spirituality*, London: SCM Press.

Farrar, Janet and Stewart ([1981], 1989), *Eight Sabbats for Witches*, London: Hale.

Farrar, Stewart ([1971], 1991), *What Witches Do: A Modern Coven Revealed*, London: Hale.

Fortune, Dion ([1956], 1994), *Moon Magic,* Maine: Samuel Weiser Inc.

Fortune, Dion ([1938], 1989), *The Sea Priestess,* Northants: Aquarian Press.

Fortune, Dion ([1935], 1987), *The Mystical Qabalah*, London: Aquarian Press.

Fox, Robin Lane (1988), *Pagans and Christians in the Mediterranean world from the second century AD to the conversion of Constantine,* Harmondsworth: Penguin.

Frazer, Sir James G. (1890), *The Golden Bough*, London: Macmillan.

Fries, Jan (1993), *Helrunar: A Manual of Rune Magick*, Oxford: Mandrake Press.

Gardner, Gerald B. ([1949], 1993), *High Magic's Aid*, London: Pentacle Enterprises.

Gardner, Gerald B. (1959), *The Meaning of Witchcraft,* London: Aquarian Press.

Gardner, Gerald B. (1954), *Witchcraft Today,* London: Rider.

Gibbons, B. J. (2001), *Spirituality and the Occult: From the Renaissance to the Modern Age*, London: Routledge.

Gilbert, R. A. (1983), *The Golden Dawn: Twilight of the Magicians*, Northants: Aquarian Press.

Gimbutas, Marija (1982), *The Goddesses and Gods of Old Europe: Myths and Cult Objects*, Berkeley: University of California Press.

Godwin, Joscelyn (1994), *The Theosophical Enlightenment*, New York: SUNY.

Goldenberg, Naomi (1979), *Changing of the Gods: Feminism and the End of Traditional Religions*, Boston: Beacon Press.

Graves, Robert (1948), *The White Goddess,* London: Faber & Faber.

Green, Marian (1991), *A Witch Alone: Thirteen Moons to Master Natural Magic*, London: Aquarian Press.

Green, Miranda (1989), *Symbol and Image in Celtic Religious Art*, London: Routledge.

Greenwood, Susan (2001), *Magic, Witchcraft and the Otherworld: An Anthropology,* Oxford: Berg.

Greer, Mary K. (1995), *Women of the Golden Dawn: Rebels and Priestesses,* Vermont: Park Street Press.

Griffin, Wendy (ed) (2000), *Daughters of the Goddess: Studies of Healing, identity and Empowerment,* California and Oxford: AltaMira.

Halifax, Joan (1982), *Shaman, the Wounded Healer,* London: Thames and Hudson.

Hanegraaff, Wouter J. (1998), *New Age Religion and Western Culture: Esotericism in the Mirror of Secular Thought,* New York: SUNY.

Harner, Michael (1990), *The way of the Shaman,* San Francisco: Harper & Row.

Harvey, Graham (1997), *Listening People, Speaking Earth: Contemporary Paganism,* London: Hurst and Co.

Harvey, Graham & Charlotte Hardman (eds) (1996), *Paganism Today: Wiccans, Druids, the Goddess and Ancient Earth Traditions for the Twenty-First Century,* London: Thorsons.

Heselton, Philip (2000), *Wiccan Roots: Gerald Gardner and the Modern Witchcraft Revival,* Berkshire: Capall Bann.

Hine, Phil (1993), *Prime Chaos,* London: Chaos International.

Hume, Lynne (1997), *Witchcraft and Paganism in Australia,* Melbourne: Melbourne University Press.

Hutton, Ronald (1999), *The Triumph of the Moon: A History of Modern Pagan Witchcraft,* Oxford: Oxford University Press.

Hutton, Ronald (1996), *The Stations of the Sun: A History of the Ritual Year in Britain,* Oxford: Oxford University Press.

Hutton, Ronald ([1991], 1993), *The Pagan Religions of the Ancient British Isles: Their Nature and Legacy,* Oxford: Blackwell.

Jones, Prudence & Caitlín Matthews (eds) (1990), *Voices From the Circle,* London: Aquarian Press.

Jones, Prudence & Nigel Pennick (1995), *A History of Pagan Europe,* London: Routledge.

Kelly, Aidan (1991), *Crafting the Art of Magic, Book 1: A History of Modern Witchcraft, 1939–1964,* St Paul, MN: Llewellyn.

King, Francis (1989), *Modern Ritual Magic: The Rise of Western Occultism,* Dorset: Prism.

Leland, Charles G. ([1899], 1998), *The New Translation of Aradia or The Gospel of the Witches,* trans. Mario & Dina Pazzaglini, Washington: Phoenix.

Lévi, Eliphas (1913), *The History of Magic* trans. A. E. Waite, London: Rider.

Lewis, James R. (ed) (1996), *Magical Religion and Modern Witchcraft,* New York: SUNY.

Lovelock, James (1982), *Gaia: A New Look at Life on Earth,* Oxford: Oxford University Press.

Luhrmann, Tanya M. ([1989], 1994), *Persuasions of the Witches' Craft: Ritual Magic in Contemporary England,* Basingstoke: Picador.

MacLellan, Gordon (1999), *Shamanism,* Piatkus.

Matthews, Caitlín and John (1994), *The Western Way: A Practical Guide to the Western Mystery Tradition,* Harmondsworth: Arkana.

Matthews, John (1991), *The Celtic Shaman,* Shaftesbury; Element.

McIntosh, Christopher (1972), *Eliphas Levi and the French Occult Revival,* London: Rider.

Murray, Margaret A. ([1933], 1970), *The God of the Witches*, London: Oxford University Press/Faber & Faber.

Murray, Margaret A. (1921), *The Witch Cult in Western Europe: A Study in Anthropology*, Oxford: Clarendon Press.

Nichols, Ross (1990), *The Book of Druidry*, London: Thorsons.

Orion, Loretta L. (1995), *Never Again the Burning Times: Paganism Revived*, Prospect Heights, Illinois: Waveland Press.

Pearson, Joanne E. (forthcoming), *Wicca: Magic, Spirituality and the 'Mystic Other'*, London: Routledge.

Pearson, Joanne E., Richard H. Roberts & Geoffrey Samuel (eds) (1998), *Nature Religion Today: Paganism in the Modern World*, Edinburgh: Edinburgh University Press.

Pike, Sarah (2001), *Earthly Bodies, Magical Selves: Contemporary Pagans and the Search for Community*, Berkeley: University of California Press.

Poole, Robert (ed) (2002), *The Lancashire Witch Trials, 1612–1999*, Manchester: Manchester University Press.

Purkiss, D. (1996), *The Witch in History: Early Modern and Twentieth Century Representations*, London: Routledge.

Regardie, Israel ([1941], 1989), *The Golden Dawn: The Original Account of the Teachings, Rites and Ceremonies of the Hermetic Order of the Golden Dawn*, St. Pauls, Minnesota: Llewellyn.

Regardie, Israel ([1932], 1973), *The Tree of Life: A Study in Magic*, New York: Samuel Weiser.

Reis, Elizabeth (ed) (1998), *Spellbound: Women and Witchcraft in America*, Wilmington, DE: Scholarly Resources Inc.

Restall Orr, Emma (1998), *Spirits of the Sacred Grove: The World of a Druid Priestess*, London: Thorsons.

Robertson, Olivia (1975), *The Call of Isis*, Neptune Press.

Russell, Jeffrey B. ([1980], 1991), *A History of Witchcraft: Sorcerers, Heretics and Pagans,* London: Thames & Hudson.

Salomonsen, Jone (2002), *Enchanted Feminism: The Reclaiming Witches of San Francisco*, London: Routledge.

Starhawk ([1979], 1989), *The Spiral Dance: A Rebirth of the Ancient Religion of the Great Goddess*, San Francisco: HarperCollins.

Thomas, Keith ([1971], 1991), *Religion and the Decline of Magic*, Harmondsworth: Penguin.

Thorsson, Edred (1991), *The Nine Doors of Midgard*, St Paul, MN: Llewellyn.

Valiente, Doreen ([1978], 1993), *Witchcraft for Tomorrow*, London: Robert Hale.

Valiente, Doreen & Evan Jones (1990), *Witchcraft: A Tradition Renewed*, Washington: Phoenix Publishing Inc.

Valiente, Doreen (1989), *The Rebirth of Witchcraft,* Washington: Phoenix Publishing Inc.

York, Michael (1995), *The Emerging Network: A Sociology of the New Age and Neo-Pagan Movements*, Maryland: Rowman and Littlefield.

2943

FOR REFERENCE
Do Not Take From This Room